PARLIAMENT HOUSE
CANBERRA
A BUILDING FOR THE NATION

PARLIAMENT HOUSE
CANBERRA
A BUILDING FOR THE NATION

EDITED BY HAIG BECK

*First published in 1988 by the New South Wales Chapter of
the Royal Australian Institute of Architects,
Tusculum, 3 Manning Street, Potts Point, Sydney, NSW.*

*National Library of Australia
Cataloguing-in-Publication data:*

*Australia's Parliament House.
Includes index.
ISBN 0 7322 0007 5.
1. Parliament House (Canberra, A.C.T.). 2. Public
buildings — Australian Capital Territory — Canberra.
3. Australia — Capital and capitol. I. Beck, Haig.
725'.11'099471*

*Typeset in Century Light by Hartland & Hyde Pty Ltd, Sydney.
Printed by The Pot Still Press, Sydney.
Colour separations by Scanagraphix, Melbourne.*

CONTENTS

I believe that history will judge the opening of Australia's new Parliament House as one of the most important events of our Bicentenary.

The design, selected in open competition amongst 329 entries from 28 countries, is a magnificent architectural concept. Its realisation is an accomplishment in excellence of which we can all be extremely proud.

Australia's first permanent Parliament House serves the dual purpose of reaffirming our commitment to democracy and providing the public with a greater opportunity to see and hear their elected representatives at work.

Aesthetically, the building complements Walter Burley Griffin's original plan for Canberra, integrating harmoniously into the layout of our national capital.

Australian materials predominate and provide a showcase of rich natural resources, moulded, shaped and fitted by the skills of 10,000 Australians from some 50 different ethnic backgrounds, who combined to realise the architects' vision.

Australia's new Parliament House reflects our confidence in the future and is a fitting symbol to take Australia into its next 200 years.

RJL Hawke
Prime Minister of Australia

FOREWORD

Everyone knows that what goes on in Parliament affects the daily lives of all Australians. The Members of Parliament debate and make decisions on how money shall be spent on defence, how much on education, on health and social services, on transport, on sport and entertainment and so on. But Parliament is not just a place where Members argue about the getting and spending of the people's money. Parliament is a place where men and women of vision tell the people what Australia might be. We have been told that without vision the people perish. The Members of Parliament are the custodians and interpreters of that vision.

In the past the great native sons and daughters of Australia have unfolded their vision. As long ago as 1823 William Charles Wentworth told Australians their destiny was to create 'a new Britannia in another world'. Nearly 70 years later Henry Parkes wanted 'the name of an Australian citizen' to 'be equal to that of the citizen of the proudest country under the sun'. At the same time Louisa Lawson wrote of women as 'the only remaining influence capable of raising humanity to a happier and nobler level'. Her son Henry Lawson urged Australians to 'banish from under their bonny skies' the 'old-world errors and wrongs and lies'. Twenty years later the young Robert Gordon Menzies exhorted his fellow-Australians to remain 'dyed in the wool British'.

Parliament House on Capital Hill is a worthy setting in which men and women can continue this never-ending debate on what Australia is and what it should be. The chief architect of the building, Romaldo Giurgola, has dreamed a great dream in keeping with the high solemnity of the work the people entrust to their elected representatives. It rises majestically from the soil of Australia. The earth of Australia and the people are one. At the entrance the Members and visitors are reminded of the long history of humanity on this continent, starting with the Aborigines, probably about 50,000 years ago. They are reminded, too, of the ideas of the Aborigines on government and of the spiritual role of the land in the life of the people. They can read of the noble aims and aspirations of others who have paved the way for the Australia of today.

The two Houses of Parliament, the House of Representatives and the Senate, are on either side of the main Members' Hall. Australia is a federation. There is a people's House and a States' House. On the flagstaff above the building flies the Australian flag. The Members have their feet on the ground, they belong to the earth. The flag on its staff reaches towards the skies. The people's representatives must be both realists and idealists. They must know the field of the possible: they must also reach for the stars. All men and women of vision must believe they can steal fire from Heaven, while they debate such mundane topics as who gets what. This building has a majesty in keeping with the high purpose of the servants of the Australian people.

Manning Clark

Manning Clark

ESSAYS

THE MAKING OF PARLIAMENT HOUSE

HAIG BECK

Parliament House, Canberra, is the seat of the Federal Government of the Commonwealth of Australia. Plans for the building were set in train on 26 August 1975, with the formation of the Joint Standing Committee on the New and Permanent Parliament House. The history of this building, however, dates from well before Federation.

Walter Burley Griffin

Neither federation of the Australian colonies on 1 January 1901 nor the designation of Canberra as site for the National Capital was a foregone conclusion. In his book *The Bush Capital*, Roger Pegrum tells how Federation was first mooted in the 1850s, but State jingoism and bitter mercantile rivalry blocked union for nearly 50 years.

By the late 1890s, early drafts of the Constitution for a federated Australia had made provision for a Parliament building, requiring the seat of government 'be within territory vested in the Commonwealth'. Just where this 'territory' would be located was to be contested for the next ten years.

In 1898, Sydneysiders were still dragging their feet over the question of Federation in the results of a State referendum on the draft Constitution. They would bear the greater financial burden of Federation. As a palliative, the draft Constitution was amended to locate the Commonwealth Territory within New South Wales. However, to avoid benefit to their rival, the Victorians insisted that the capital be not located within 100 miles of Sydney.

In New South Wales a Royal Commission was established in 1899 to find a suitable territory of 100 square miles for the seat of government of the Commonwealth of Australia. Sites in three regions were favoured by the Commission. Debate, visits to the regions by politicians, and more debate followed. The site called Yass-Canberra was chosen by the House of Representatives in the ninth ballot on 9 October 1908. It was surveyed and an international competition for the new capital was proposed finally in 1911.

In setting up terms for the competition, the Government's Minister for Home Affairs reserved the right to reject or amend the jury's decision. Maps, models, and sketches were displayed in Australia, New Zealand, South Africa, Canada, the USA, Britain, France, and Germany. Prizes of £1,750, £750, and £500 were offered, and 137 entries received. The chairman of the jury could not agree on a result with the other two judges. However, as Pegrum notes, in a move for which Australia must be forever thankful, the Minister accepted the majority verdict and selected the design of Walter Burley Griffin.

Griffin, aged 35, was from Chicago. He had been chief assistant of the formidable Frank Lloyd Wright, in whose office Griffin met his wife, Marion Mahony (who rendered the winning entry). The design brilliantly combined the vision of a garden city with the natural topography, aligning the principal boulevards on distant vistas and gathering the city's centre around the shores of an artificial lake. Government buildings were set out in a triangle overlooking the lake (now called the Parliamentary Triangle and Lake Burley Griffin). At the apex of the triangle is Capital Hill. Griffin designated the site just under it for the Houses of Parliament.

Though much admired, Griffin's plan also drew sniping and penny-pinching criticisms. The government prepared its own design, the Departmental Board Plan. It was an ill-conceived mishmash that was immediately and widely denounced. When Griffin arrived in Australia in 1913, he was appointed Federal Capital Director of Design and Construction. His first task was to rescue his original design.

For the next seven years (until he resigned the post in 1920), Griffin faced a constant battle of back-biting intrigues and administrative delays as he fought to implement his plan. An international competition was announced for the new Parliament House, but cancelled on the outbreak of war in 1914. Griffin did, however, get his plan for Canberra approved in 1918 (it was finally gazetted in 1925); and, before resigning, he had laid out the city's radiating boulevards that now define the Parliamentary Triangle and give the older suburbs of Canberra their distinctive character.

In 1923 an Australia-wide competition was held for a temporary (provisional) Parliament House. It was won by the Sydney architect G Sydney Jones and the building completed in 1927. Thereafter Canberra languished until 1954 when a Parliamentary Select Committee was set up to report on the development of the National Capital — then a country town of 35,000 people, with sheep still grazing on what has become the lake.

The provisional building of 1927 had been designed to accommodate 75 Members of the House of Representatives and 36 Senators. By the mid-1970s these numbers had doubled. The need for a new Parliament House was becoming urgent, and so the Joint Standing Committee was formed.

The siting of the new building was hotly debated in Parliament. It was proposed to locate it on Griffin's original site on Camp Hill (a small rise just below Capital Hill) before settling on Capital Hill itself in 1978. This decision raised eyebrows, as Griffin had designated Capital Hill as a public park and meeting place, symbolically locating the people above Parliament. (Griffin's gesture, though, is cleverly retained in the new building.)

In late 1978 the Parliament House Construction Authority was formed to manage the design and construction of a new building. A two-stage competition was held, drawing 329 entries from 28 countries. The selected design by Mitchell/Giurgola & Thorp — a unanimous choice of the jury — was announced on 26 June 1980.

Mitchell/Giurgola were a well-established practice of American architects with offices in New York and Philadelphia. Ehrman

■ *Marion Mahony Griffin's rendering of Walter Burley Griffin's winning design for the new capital (1912).*

B Mitchell Jr, the retiring American partner of the practice and Romaldo Giurgola, born and trained in Rome, along with their younger partners, had formed a partnership for the competition with Richard Thorp, a young Australian, working in the New York office.

The opening of the new building was set for 1988 to coincide with Australia's bicentennial celebration of European settlement: leaving just under eight years to design and erect a building with the floor area of three skyscrapers, the technical complexity of a general hospital and which had to be executed with the nobility of finishes appropriate to the nation's most significant monument.

To undertake this mammoth task two of the country's largest building and civil engineering groups — Concrete Constructions and John Holland — pooled resources to form the Concrete-Holland Joint Venture. (Their proposal was one of 80 submitted to the Construction Authority by Australian and international companies.)

The original cost estimate in 1978 for the bare building was $220 million. To this is added the fitting out costs, accommodation additional to the original brief, and the effects of inflation, bringing the total budget to just over $1,000 million at 1988 values.

A conventional fixed-price contract based on traditional tendering procedures was out of the question: to prepare all the drawings, details, and specifications before selecting a builder and commencing construction wouldn't leave enough time to finish the building by the 1988 deadline. The Construction Authority proposed instead a 'construction management' contract in which the contractor was to be paid a fixed sum to manage the construction.

This enabled the Authority to appoint the Concrete-Holland Joint Venture as construction manager before the results of the architectural competition were even known. The architects' competition entry was refined and presented to Parliament. Simultaneously, an overall budget was prepared based on an independent quantity surveyor's cost estimates.

Less than 18 months after the competition results had been announced, the first of more than 500 sub-contracts had been let and construction was under way. This swift start was made possible by a radical new management procedure called 'fast-tracking'. Construction begins as soon as the architect's work has progressed sufficiently for the structural engineer to design the foundations. So that the architects and their technical consultants can keep ahead of the builders, a timetable is prepared that schedules each step of the building process.

Fast-tracking has been used mainly for large civil engineering projects (dams, powerstations and the like) and commercial developments (office buildings and factories) where questions of beauty (aesthetics) are secondary — if considered at all. The structure is erected first and the services and claddings installed later. Cables, pipes, and ducts are clipped onto the structural carcase and the whole mess covered up with suspended ceilings, computer floors, and drywalling. The architectural treatment of these 'skins' is so often dumb and mechanistic: sheer cliffs of mirror glass, acres of metal decking, corridors of prefabricated partitions. While the process of fast-tracking was essential to the timed completion of the building, these mass-produced materials with their commercial/industrial connotations were not suitable finishes for Parliament House.

Mitchell/Giurgola & Thorp's solution to this has antecedents in ancient Roman building techniques. The Greeks built their temples and civic monuments solidly in marble — every block had to be skilfully carved by highly trained masons. The Romans realized that a wall didn't have to be solid marble — a thin skin of this expensive material could be fixed over a much cheaper wall of brickwork or concrete to give the same effect.

The Romans, with characteristic efficiency, divided construction into two stages with separate building teams. Workers on the first team — responsible for the structural carcase — were mostly unskilled labourers. Only the second team that followed behind applying the fine architectural finishes required skilled artisans. This highly rationalized approach to building was also used by the Romans to reduce construction time — with the marble cladding being prepared in workshops away from the site while the carcase was still going up: an early form of fast-tracking.

Like many Roman buildings, under the smooth surfaces of Parliament House is a massive core of concrete (300,000 cubic metres of it — enough to build 25 Sydney Opera Houses). While the concrete was being poured for the huge curved walls, the granite cladding — 24,000 slabs from Eugowra in central New South Wales — was simultaneously being cut and honed on computer-controlled machines especially developed for the task.

Each granite panel was cut precisely: the specification demanded accuracy to within one millimetre. On the other hand, forming the concrete walls behind was, necessarily, a cruder process: much greater variations were deemed acceptable — any mismatch being taken up by adjustable steel fixing brackets. This technique is used throughout Parliament House for mounting the masonry, timber, or fabric panels that clad much of the building.

A simple, but ingenious solution of using brackets whose dimensions varied was devised by the architects to support these materials. The brackets added, in effect, a third (middle) stage to the ancient Roman building system. After the structural carcase was in place (and while all the cables, pipes, and ducts were being installed), the brackets were positioned with packing to eradicate the effects of any bumps and hollows in the wall behind. At the same time, teams of craftsmen confident of perfectly levelled fixings were fabricating panels of finely finished timberwork and polished stone in workshops scattered all over Australia (and as far away as Italy).

■ *Romaldo Giurgola's rendering of Parliament House for Mitchell/Giurgola & Thorp's winning design (1980).*

The urgency of the fast-track programme was such that construction of the structural carcase often had to proceed long before the surface treatment had been decided or runs of cables and pipes had been planned. To accommodate virtually any finish or combination of services, a gap was designed between the structural carcase and the internal surfaces of the building (this gap also tolerated the imprecisions of concrete construction). At floor level a space of 150mm suited timber, parquetry, marble, tiles,·and carpet alike; only 100mm was needed for the walls; 1 metre in the ceilings would hide even the large air-conditioning ducts.

The practical and aesthetic possibilities of fabricating highly-crafted architectural finishes away from the site under controlled workshop conditions are tremendous. Traditional on-site techniques are more labour-intensive, time-consuming, and less flexible.

Fast-tracking and the scale of the Parliament House project have initiated a new era of craftsmanship in Australia, deploying new materials, new methods, new tools. Several native materials have been used in unexpected contexts throughout the building: timbers like turpentine in the Members' Hall and grey box joinery in the House of Representatives chamber are examples.

Green is the traditional colour of the House of Representatives. In choosing colours for the new chamber, the architects were inspired by the grey-greens of the Australian bush, using them for the fabric wall panels and leather upholstered parliamentary benches. They wanted a brown timber with a cool grey hue for the joinery in the chamber, but the only readily available native timbers were flushed with hot pinks or warm yellows.

Mitchell/Giurgola & Thorp's research turned up grey box, which had been previously ignored by the joinery industry as a hardwood only fit for railway sleepers and fenceposts.

The search for a suitable timber to clad the columns in the Members' Hall led to turpentine. It had the right colour and fine-grained density, but was too unstable for joinery work (resistant to marine attack, it has been used mainly for building wharves and bridges). This sort of challenge was typical of problems which Concrete Holland's Quality Assurance Group regarded as opportunities. Under their guidance, effective new kiln-monitoring procedures were developed to stabilize the moisture content — and so another native timber (and possibly others too) has been introduced to the Australian joinery industry.

Parliament House is pervaded by this attention to detail, a collaboration between the architects and the Quality Assurance Group. The building's finishes are the result of a constant pursuit of aesthetic quality and the technical demands of durability. The perfect granite for the Forecourt paving was finally found on the edge of the Great Australian Bight — a new type of masonry saw bench was devised to mass-produce the thousands of stones required. The pergolas were made from jarrah over 100 years old — rescued just in time from a woolshed being demolished in Fremantle. Much of the specially designed furniture was handcrafted from a cache of rare Australian timbers — offered by an enthusiast who had collected them over a lifetime.

Since the best Australian marbles had not been quarried to good effect, imported marbles had to be used. The architects and the construction manager scrutinized Italian quarries, identifying material while it was still in the ground. (The exquisitely figured and matched panels of white marble that clad the Forecourt portico show the most visible result of this effort.)

Normally the urgencies of fast-tracking severely restrict aesthetic options: there just isn't time, resources, or inclination to research and develop better alternatives. On the new Parliament House, fast-tracking has actually extended the architects' choice of materials and finishes. This is partly accounted for by the flexibility of their system for attaching the architectural finishes and the relatively long time-scale of such a major project. The clinching factor, however, has been the overall effect of the Quality Assurance Group.

The Group was established by the Concrete-Holland Joint Venture with wide terms of reference for ensuring consistently high standards. This commitment to excellence permeated a workforce 10,000 strong (with some 2,000 people on site at any one time). Its consequences include the minimal labour disruption and unparalleled safety record which attended construction of Parliament House. More significantly, workmanship everywhere in the building exhibits a spirit of pride and excellence.

The construction industry and the architectural profession can greatly benefit from the example of Parliament House. Together, Concrete-Holland and Mitchell/Giurgola & Thorp have unleashed the creative managerial and aesthetic potentials of fast-tracking. The quality of architectural finishes they have achieved constitutes a revival in craftsmanship that had practically vanished in the wake of machine-made, mass-produced materials and building techniques. The labour record on Parliament House and its completion on time suggest that the internecine warfare that generally passes for industrial relations on many sites is unnecessary.

Australia will not build another Parliament House, but the architectural principles, construction techniques, and building practices nurtured here can apply to nearly any major commercial or public building project. If this occurs, Australians will be better off.

THE ARCHITECTURE OF PARLIAMENT HOUSE

HAIG BECK

The first thing you see is the flag.

Remember the holiday excitement of that first glimpse of the sea? Who would think such a small blue patch in the distance could shimmer with so many associations? It is just the same with the flag that flutters above Canberra's new parliamentary complex.

It is impossible to approach Parliament House without expectations. The building is as much an emblem of Australia as the Opera House is of Sydney. Yet the drive over the lake and up the sides of the Parliamentary Triangle discloses a paradox: there is no building — just a flag, a hill, and a wall.

The idea 'Australia' is distilled in three quintessential signs: the flag, emblem of nationhood; the hill, embodiment of place; and the wall, mark of human inhabitation. These abstract yet highly representational signs prompt individual feelings about patriotism, place, people.

Parliamentarians and the public alike approach Parliament House along the arms of the Parliamentary Triangle. As they draw closer to the building, their paths and perceptions divide: visitors enter from the north; Members of the House of Representatives from the east; Ministers from the south; and Senators from the west. The diagonal approach across the Canberra landscape shifts onto the building's axes. The abstract collage of flag, hill, and wall becomes realigned in a more figurative composition. Viewed on axis, the supporting legs of the flag-mast outline a pyramidal form: a 'roof' of childlike simplicity (or abstracted cupola?).

Each entrance is different. On the north is a monumental marbled portico that welcomes visitors. The Prime Minister's entrance to the Executive domain on the opposite side of the building has an altogether more humble architectural treatment with a 'front' door. Entry to the House of Representatives is from a porte cochère, austerely composed, its solid roof based on the geometry of the square, with decorative inlays of green marbles. (Green traditionally signifies the Lower House, red the Upper.) On the Senate side, the porte cochère form is sumptuous, the geometry circular, the roof glazed, and the marble inlays red.

The differences are not arbitrary. Architectural inversions (big portico/little door, green square/red circle) are opposed to make distinctions which are geographic (north/south, east/west); programmatic (public/private, Member/Senator); and symbolic (citizens/elected leader, 'lower' house/'upper' house).

Portico, porte cochère, and front door all signify 'formal entrance'. Each has particular status and meaning according to the experience of entry conventionally associated with it. A portico signifies an important public entrance; a porte cochère is less public and approached by vehicle; a front door, relative to the other two, is a private entrance.

At Parliament House, symbolic and functional distinctions are

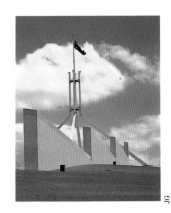

■ *Flag, hill, wall*

■ *Flag, hill, walls on axis*

■ *Executive entrance*

■ *House of Representatives porte cochère*

■ *Senate porte cochère*

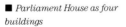
■ *Parliament House as four buildings*

made among the several formal entrances to the building. A portico heralds the public ceremonial entrance from the north. In contrast, the front door to the Executive denotes an entrance that is private. The approaches to the two Houses are by vehicle, off-axis up the long flanks of the facade. Projecting portes cochères make these entrances legible and also indicate vehicle drop-off points.

Legibility is essential in the building which is bigger than most small towns. With both Houses sitting, upwards of 3,500 people will occupy nearly 4,000 rooms. Daily, 5,000 visitors are expected, and a further 1,500 must be catered for on State occasions. A prodigious support network is necessary.

Beneath Parliament House spreads a vast subterranean realm of car parks, plant rooms, workshops, and kitchens. The grid of corridors is festooned with pipeways, cable trunking, and air-conditioning ducts. Through this maze threads a sophisticated communications network: cable TV and telecommunications, a documents 'train' that stops at 30-odd stations, a facsimile service, and — for occasions when the ink of a minister's signature must be sighted — even a pneumatic tube system.

Above ground, people constitute the parliamentary support system. The media have to be accommodated, Hansard housed, people fed. Officers and staff of the two Houses, ushers and guides, maintenance crews and messengers all require work stations. There are places for work (libraries and committee rooms) and places for play (dining areas and recreational facilities). For the public there is an auditorium, post office, and cafeteria. Mundane necessities like security posts, store rooms, and toilets must be located intelligibly.

Offices for 127 of the 148 Members are on the eastern side of Parliament. Suites for 67 of the 76 Senators (and Hansard) are on the west. The remaining 30 Members and Senators are in the Executive wing to the south, poised between the two Houses. Here are the Prime Minister's offices, Cabinet room, Ministers' suites, libraries, media studios, and committee rooms.

Inside this mini-metropolis of human and technological activity, all industry is dedicated to the smooth functioning of the two chambers. In them speeches are made, questions asked, motions debated, and legislation enacted. Voting is the crucial act: on the sounding of the division bell, parliamentarians have four minutes to drop whatever they are doing, no matter where they are in the building, and go to their chamber and vote. For those who miss a critical vote, getting lost on the way to the chamber is not an excuse as far as Party Whips are concerned.

This necessity — that MPs be able to find their way around Parliament — is extended to include everyone who visits the building. Sensing the symbolic meanings of its parts is as important as knowing where you are within the complex. The building has to be legible in terms of its geography, its functions, and its symbolism.

Architecture provides more than functional shelter. It creates backdrops for activities and experiences, which over time may become so strongly associated with their architectural settings that the built form comes to signify the experience. This semiotic principle applies to Parliament House. Its four main activities (functions) are geographically isolated and given their own architectural settings — internally and externally.

In anthropomorphic terms, the building has a front, back, and sides. The setting for Parliament's public ceremonial functions is at the front, straddling Walter Burley Griffin's imposing Land Axis — Canberra's ceremonial spine focused on the War Memorial. Parliament and Memorial are axially locked in an urban-scaled symbolic dialogue about patriotism (Memorial) and nationhood (Parliament). The sense of Australia as place is firmly embedded in the way that these symbols are seen to be rooted in the soil. The ceremonial axis is terminated in the land at each end, by Mount Ainslie and Capital Hill.

From the front, Parliament House appears carved into the living rock of Capital Hill. To enter Parliament — enter the hill — is to enter 'Australia'. Among architecture's most powerfully sustained evocations of genius loci are the rock-cut monuments of ancient civilizations: the tombs of Petra, the Great Tomb at Abu-Simbel, the Treasury at Arteus, Mycenae. The most impressive, the Temple of Queen Hatshepsut in Upper Egypt — its trabeated portico stretching in front of the cliffs of Thebes — could almost be a prototype for the front of Parliament House. Seen from outside, the architectural setting for Parliament's public ceremonial functions is abstracted into three simple, memorable forms: the flag, the excavated embrace of Capital Hill, and the screen wall of the Great Verandah. The elements that read from the distance — flag, hill, and wall — are viewed here in a new and more stable configuration.

Discrete buildings house the other principal activities of Parliament. The Executive is out the back. It is a solid, austere, foursquare block, expressing the *gravitas* of the office of Prime Minister. Lodged into the side of Capital Hill, the Executive (read 'Prime Minister') is placed symbolically in direct contact with 'Australia'.

The two Houses flanked by attendant offices are located at the sides. The free-standing Houses are plainly office buildings. However, the typical rows of anonymous, serial office windows are modulated by piers to designate each parliamentarian's suite of rooms. At night, light from the tops of the chambers signals across Canberra when the Houses are in session. By day, the chambers are identified by their terra-cotta tiled roofs. They are synonymous with the red tiled roofs of Australian suburbia and invite symbolic interpretation.

This is the 'business' end of Parliament — in contrast to the public ceremonial front of white marbled portico, magnificent polished granite walls, and gleaming stainless steel flag supports. The

22

■ *Great Tomb, Abu-Simbel*

■ *Temple of Queen Hatshepsut, Upper Egypt*

■ *Treasury at Arteus, Mycenae*

■ *Terra-cotta roof on the House of Representatives chamber*

detailing and finishes of these three buildings are almost utilitarian: sand-blasted precast panels modestly articulated with marble inlays.

The physical separation of Parliament into four buildings is achieved by two sweeping granite-clad curved walls. Like a sculptor's armature, they structure the entire composition. They are massive retaining walls carving into Capital Hill to reveal its 'contours' in profile, providing a base for the flag and a backdrop for the two Houses. Between the walls are the remains of the hill. Two excavations of its lower slopes form the Forecourt on one side and a setting for the Executive on the other.

The walls are more than functional. They are overlaid with cultural signs that express aesthetics, intention, and technical skill. The geometric stepped outlines are sharply delineated against the expanse of the sky; controlled views of the countryside beyond are framed in 'window' cut-outs; granite facings are finely honed with mechanized precision. The understated opulence of the granite finishes contrasts with the severity of the precast cladding on the two Houses below — underlining the distinction between the business side of Parliament and the public, ceremonial, and symbolic realms.

The arcs described by the walls on the landscape gesture far beyond the boundaries of the site. On the northern side of Capital Hill they spread to gather the sides of the Parliamentary Triangle to an apex — the flag. Viewed from under the flag, Griffin's plan for Canberra is laid out across the Molonglo valley. Urban geometry and natural topography together generate a majestic sense of Canberra as a place, with Parliament House at its centre. Radiating boulevards divide and order the valley floor, the Land Axis orients the city at Mount Ainslie, and the Water Axis — Lake Burley Griffin — establishes the base of the Parliamentary Triangle.

The organizing form of the curved walls sets Parliament House at the centre of a much wider stage that appropriates the national capital and surrounding countryside. The flag, hill, walls, city — even the land — synergetically act to signify 'Parliament', each contributing its own rich store of connotations and associations.

Inside Parliament House, each important public, parliamentary, and ceremonial function occupies its own setting. The public ceremonial route traces the line of the Land Axis through a series of linked rooms, culminating at the core of Parliament under the flag. Each space along the route is different. Each is made a memorable venue for the activity it contains.

The spaces are orchestrated as an ensemble — a set-piece. This architectural tableau begins at the Forecourt, a vast outdoor 'room'. Framed on three sides, it is a public gathering place. The connotations of the sunburnt-red space and its central 'leafy' pool are of deserts and billabongs — a nostalgic and mythologized image of Australia as place. This Aboriginal reading is reinforced by a large mos-

■ *Griffin's topographic vision for Canberra realized*

■ *The Forecourt as outdoor 'room'*

aic at the centre of the pool, a Papunya ground painting (transposed into coloured granite sets) depicting the gathering of clans.

The portico billows out in an expansive gesture of welcome. Visitors are propelled towards it by the spatial dynamics of the angled sides of the Forecourt, the physical imperative of the Land Axis, and the focusing effect of the flag.

The portico is planar, square-cut, and trabeated; the cladding (square marble panels) is white; a tripartite set of openings (surmounted by a coat of arms) marks the entry. The references to Provisional Parliament House — though abstracted — are inescapable. There are even five upper-storey 'windows' in the colonnaded screen walls to each side.

For many Australians, televised interviews with politicians on the front steps of Provisional Parliament House have been their most immediate experience of the parliamentary process. The white portico is backdrop to these small screen dramas; a fleeting shot of the facade is television news shorthand for 'parliamentary item follows'. The Great Verandah of the new building recalls the forms of its predecessor in order to invest it with similar associations.

Abstraction makes the new portico both familiar and different: it carries connotations of historical past and contemporary modernism. The other memorable venues of Provisional Parliament House — King's Hall and the two chambers — are similarly recalled in the new building. A sense of continuity of the culture and the Constitution is evident, of time passing and of things changing yet remaining constant in certain essentials.

The route into Parliament House emerges through the portico under a shady glazed roof. This place, marking the transition between inside and out, is immediately understood as an Australian form: a Great Verandah. Just inside the grand portico facade is a simple single-storey wall with a wisteria-draped loggia above, thronged with people. Here perception of Parliament changes: the monumentality of the Forecourt and Capital Hill is exchanged for a more intimate and human scale.

Perception is always related to human experience and measure. We make sense of buildings by using ourselves and previous experiences as yardsticks. The subliminal (and frequently anthropomorphic) associations automatically invoked to link experiences with the places they occur in can be harnessed and directed to make buildings more legible — and therefore memorable. There needs to be evidence of human scale, inhabitation, and craft. These signs can be read in the entrance wall to Parliament House: the low, broad 'head-and-shoulders' form of the doorway elegantly faced in marble, and its flanking windows and marbled balustrade above.

Inside the doorway is the Foyer, a marble floor studded with columns. In the space of a few metres the sense of Parliament House as a place is radically altered: invocations of the physical presence of

■ *Provisional Parliament House*

■ *Entrance loggia*

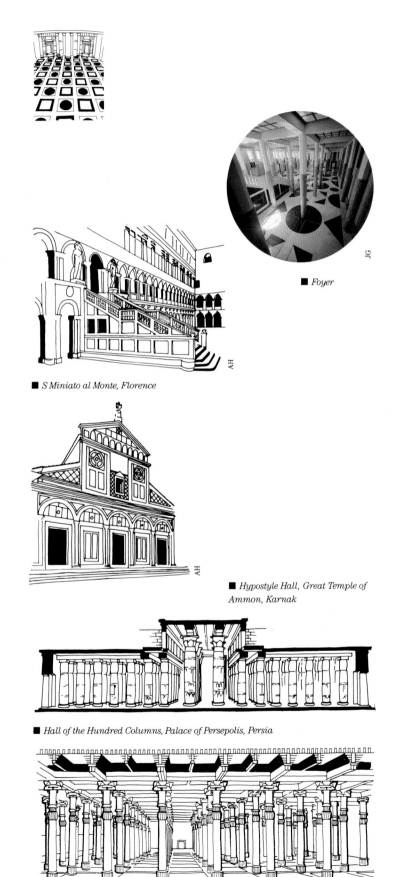

■ *Foyer*

■ *S Miniato al Monte, Florence*

■ *Hypostyle Hall, Great Temple of Ammon, Karnak*

■ *Hall of the Hundred Columns, Palace of Persepolis, Persia*

the 'hill' and the 'natural' landscape are supplanted by references that belong to the traditions of architecture and the reality of Parliament as a building. A grey-green forest of marble columns divides and regulates the Foyer, clearing a space to form a central processional way. The columns are natural magnets where people gather and meet. Coloured geometric patterns order the marble floor and calibrate the height of columns. North light from behind the mezzanine floods into the top of the Foyer, bouncing off the gridded ceiling and the white plaster tops of the column shafts.

The entrance wall outside is remembered in the precast wall panels and mezzanine balustrade in the Foyer. A marquetry frieze depicting indigenous flora brings inside the 'Australian' symbolism that characterizes the Forecourt. The experience of the Foyer, however, is altogether European.

The bold marble floor recalls geometric paving in the Pantheon, Rome; the stairs to each side of the processional axis rework the Scala del Giganti in the Grand Cortile of the Doge's Palace, Venice; decorating the staircase sides are marble inlays that suggest the facade of the Romanesque church S Miniato al Monte, Florence. The architectural references are not exclusively Italian. The many-columned hall preceded by a forecourt has ancient antecedents: the Hypostyle Hall of the Great Temple of Ammon, Karnak, and the Hall of the Hundred Columns in the Palace of Persepolis, Persia. Collectively, the references invoke the architecture of western civilization.

The Foyer and the Forecourt are the two primary public spaces of Parliament House. Their contrasting architectural treatments reflect the essential dichotomy of Australia as a people: expressions of a European 'universal' culture inside are juxtaposed against those of 'aboriginal' Australia outside.

The public and ceremonial routes separate in the Foyer. Except on State occasions the doors to the Great Hall beyond remain closed, their presence lost in the pattern of wall panelling. The two staircases are the central feature. Their purpose is clearly to entice visitors up to the balustraded mezzanine and towards the light.

From here into the building beyond, visitors are restricted to the first floor. They can watch (and be seen watching) Parliament's principal activities: State receptions in the Great Hall; the bustle of parliamentarians and their assistants through the Members' Hall; the cut-and-thrust of debate in the two chambers.

The spatial tableau and symbolic narrative of the ceremonial route through the building continues on the ground floor into the Great Hall, where the 'European' material of the Foyer — marble — gives way to Australian timbers. European signs are still evident — chiefly the colonnade of squared pillars interspersed with paired columns lining the two sides of the room. Yet the timber panelling, parquet flooring, and top lighting are more redolent of the atmosphere of King's Hall in Provisional Parliament House or of a Federation

25

period Australian dining room (though on a sufficiently grand scale to seat 800 for a State dinner).

The timber wall panelling, which is based on ‘a door-sized module, mediates between the immense room and the people in it. The human-related dimensions of the panelling establish a scale for the room. Contrasting edging timbers delineate the proportions, shadow lines highlight the thickness of the wood, and the grain, seen and felt, exploits the tactile pleasures of timber. The panelling — familiar, measurable, memorable — is a cipher for ‘reading’ the room. It also has a very practical purpose: to camouflage doors to the service areas. Above the centre of this cavernous volume is a giant roof monitor that draws light down into the room.

The spaces along the ceremonial procession into the depths of the building are linked by an axis. The architectural treatment of daylight along the route also emphasizes the sequential quality of the route. A narrative in natural light expresses progressive penetration into the building: from the almost blinding sky-dome of the Forecourt, through the shaded Great Verandah, into the bright north-lit Foyer, and on to the subdued luminance of the Great Hall, where light filters down through a shaft cut into the ceiling. The changing quality of the light enhances the legibility and comprehension of the route and its linked places.

After the dimness of the Great Hall, the ceremonial route bursts out into the light again to arrive in the atrium space of the Members’ Hall. It occupies the geographical centre of Parliament House, directly under the flag and at the crossroads between people and Prime Minister along one axis and the two Houses along the other. The sequence of this route (and of every archetypal journey) follows the schema light–dark–light (Paradise–The Fall–Salvation). Its significance and appeal are universal.

Giant portals — like colossi over the four entrances into the Members’ Hall — frame the space. Lest there is any confusion about these being ‘doors’, the abstracted head-and-shoulders doorway form of the front entrance is repeated, but exploded to monumental scale. No other doors are distinguished by such oversized proportions, vaunted beyond the human scale to proclaim the emblematic significance of this place. The three-storey-high cut-outs reveal the ‘door-portals’ as free-standing screen walls. The pattern of stepped incisions demarcates the three floors of Parliament House and leads the eye towards the rooflight and the flag flying above.

The four portal-cum-screen walls can be perceived as a single entity. Collectively they assume the form of a *baldacchino* (a canopy over an altar, usually supported on columns): four sets of paired columns rise over an ‘altar’ of black granite to support a glazed pyramid canopy. The square of black granite at the centre of the Members’ Hall contains a pool reflecting the sky and flag above. Flag, earth, sky, and water (emblems of nationhood and place) converge on the

26

■ *Great Hall*

■ *Members’ Hall*

■ *Baldacchino, St Peter’s, Rome*

THE ARCHITECTURE OF PARLIAMENT HOUSE

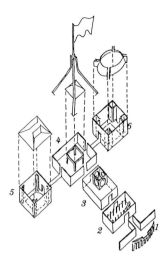

■ *The spatial tableau*

Key: 1 *Portico*
2 *Foyer*
3 *Great Hall*
4 *Members' Hall*
5 *House chamber*
6 *Senate chamber*

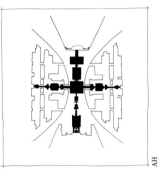

■ *Ceremonial axis*

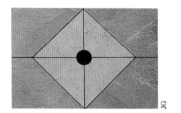

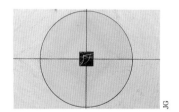

■ *Red-green shift*

■ *Capitol, Washington DC*

one plane at the centre of Parliament.

The tableau of spaces along the ceremonial path into Parliament House chronicles an abbreviated history of Australia: it spans from the Aboriginal dreamtime (Forecourt), the period of European arrival (Foyer), Federation (Great Hall), to the present (Members' Hall). Contemporaneity is suggested by the toing and froing of parliamentarians, the fluctuating light levels as clouds pass over, and the constantly flickering flag reflected in the pool. (This history is architectonically projected into the future as the axis continues south through the Cabinet Room and the Main Committee Room — the venues of decisions that determine national destiny.)

Similar (though symbolically less elaborate) tableaux of spaces provide a memorable order to the ceremonial paths into the two Houses. This 'Constitutional' cross-axis is an architectural metaphor for the bicameral parliamentary system which balances the two Houses (expressed in the chambers) around the Constitution (the Members' Hall). The routes pass from portes cochères, through foyers, stair hall, Speaker's and President's entrance halls and courtyards, chamber foyers, and finally into the Members' Hall. Each space along the route has a specific ambience, and each ensemble of spaces builds to a special architectural character for each House. Distinctions between the Upper and Lower Houses are made in terms of colour (red/green), geometry (circles/squares), and sumptuary rules (lavish/spare).

The prominence of red and circles identifies the Senate: red marble inlays at the entrance, pink walls inside, red fabrics, carpet, and leather in the chambers. Circular forms characterize the porte cochère, entrance stairs, lightwell above the chamber foyer, and the chamber itself. The tangible luxuriousness in the 'upper' House is expressed in sensual curves, rich reds, and the grandeur of the President's Courtyard with a great arched upper storey and substantial colonnaded covered way.

The 'lower' House is more austere, characterized by its sober square geometry, traditional greens, and a simple tin-roofed, timber-framed, verandah-like shelter across the Speaker's Courtyard.

For the visitor to Parliament House, the location and legibility of the two chambers are clarified through another architectural tableau in which the chambers are axially linked via glazed bridges to opposite sides of the Members' Hall. From the glazed bridges the full sweep of the curved walls is revealed, the chambers recognized as discrete buildings, and much of the geography of the Parliament complex made apparent.

As well as the very obvious red/green distinctions between the two chambers, there are also architectonic differences that contribute to their particular and separate identities. Each chamber is surmounted by a 'dome', which traditionally marks a space of great civic or ceremonial importance (the dome of the American Capitol comes

27

to mind). Here they are abstracted (this is the late 20th century): a truncated pyramid rises over the square ceiling of the House of Representatives. At each corner, the pyramid is carried on paired columns that stand proud of the chamber walls. Light filters into the chamber around the base of the pyramid, intimating a second, outer roof above it. The pyramid and its supporting columns appear to form a free-standing 'canopied' structure within the chamber — another *baldacchino*, used here to add significance and weight to the proceedings below.

■ *Chamber 'dome', House of Representatives*

■ *Chamber 'dome', Senate*

The Senate chamber ceiling is very different. Its truncated conical dome has no visible supports: suffused with light, it floats above an encircling band of dark glass. At the corners of the chamber back-lit glazed slits — not columns — rise up: the roof is held aloft by four 'negative' columns of light.

Seating in the chambers continues the familiar horseshoe arrangement of Provisional Parliament House. This layout for debating has antecedents in the democratic institutions of Classical Greece — the *bouleutorions* (council houses).

Unlike Provisional Parliament House — where the visitors' galleries overhang the floors of the chambers — spectators have an unrestricted view of proceedings below. The relationship between the public and parliamentarians is subtly, but significantly, altered. Whereas the public galleries in Provisional Parliament House were relatively out of sight (and out of mind?), in the new chambers, parliamentarians are at centre stage (a metaphor reinforced by the proscenium-like frame to the galleries in the House of Representatives), and visually engaged with an audience which now includes the public as well as other politicians.

The axial route through the Executive building is also arranged in an architectural tableau of entrances, antechambers, and rooms. It connects Prime Minister and Cabinet to the Members' Hall. Like the other paths, it is more symbolic than functional. Doors exist to provide uninterrupted passage through the spaces along each axis to the centre of the building, but protocol and security dictate that these paths are not generally part of the everyday circulation.

The symbolic ceremonial routes bestow meaning and geographic order to the parts of the building. But everyday circulation patterns need to be more pragmatic. People have to reach every part of the building swiftly and without getting lost.

Internal 'streets' criss-cross the building from north-south and east-west. Mapping a way through this grid is surprisingly easy: each corridor terminates in light at the perimeter of the building; each intersection along the way is a 'place' with a distinctive character; green or red identify the east and west sides respectively; art and craft works and glimpses of the curved walls, courtyards, Foyer, flag, and chambers provide additional reference points and markers.

Familiar architectural elements in constant use — doors, win-

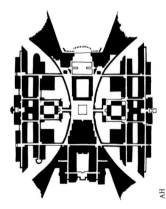

■ *A grid of internal 'streets'*

28

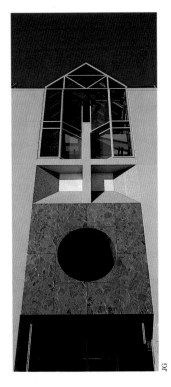

■ *Executive entrance*

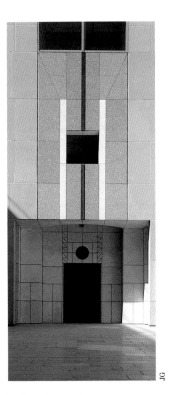

■ *Prime Minister's entrance*

■ *Parliamentary wing office suites*

■ *'Trabeated' facade to the Executive Courtyard*

dows, stairs — are given special treatment. The experience of using them is made memorable, so that each becomes associated with a particular place or type of activity in the building.

The entrance doors to the office suites of Members and Senators are all the same, but given precedence over other doors in the corridors by their larger size, the pronounced thickness of the frame, and a glazed panel that reveals the receptionist in a room behind. Doors to ministerial suites are more imposing: full-height, double-leafed, and timber-veneered.

Important openings along the two major axes take their cue from the tripartite head-and-shoulders form of the front entrance portico. Variations include: three doorways (front entrance), columns (Senate porte cochère); and doors in combination with timber panelling (Great Hall), windows (Prime Minister's suite), niches (cabinet suite).

The Executive entrance, and beyond it the Prime Minister's entrance at the end of the Executive Courtyard — though merely doors in a wall — appropriate the entire facade to achieve a three-part configuration and give the necessary status to their function. These entrances are quite different from each other, yet clearly related through a series of architectural inversions that plays on circles and squares and red and green marble inlays. (These 'signs' of the two Houses are present, no doubt, to suggest that the Executive draws on the combined resources of both Houses to govern.)

The windows of Parliament House are not only for looking out of and for letting light in. They frame views, regulate light levels, signal the type of activity that occurs behind them (and indicate the presence of people), help establish a human-related scale, and reveal something of a wall's mass and structure.

The long wings of the two Houses obviously accommodate office suites: the size and serial rhythm of windows recall many low-rise office buildings. Similar windows in the Executive Courtyard identify Ministers' office suites. Above them the pattern changes to a frieze of small square openings surmounted by a few much larger windows belonging to the library. The smaller, desk-height, windows limit glare while giving readers intimate views. The larger windows — well above head-height — open only to the sky: they bathe the room in reflected light.

The combined effect of the windows down the sides of the Executive Courtyard gives the two walls the appearance of a giant trabeated colonnade. The large area of windows of the lower two floors suggests the 'openings' in the colonnade, the piers between office suites are the 'columns', and the relatively solid wall of the library above is the 'beam' they support.

Trabeation is a very simple structural form: everyone senses how beams are held up by columns. It gives a reassuring sense of structural substance to the courtyard walls — an idea of how they

29

stand up. This expression of legible 'structure' recurs throughout Parliament House: in the Forecourt portico, portes cochères, the facades of the two Houses and the Executive, the Great Hall, and the portals in the Members' Hall.

In the front entrance wall, small head-height windows are punched through to signify the mass of masonry. In contrast to the monumental approach to Parliament House, the windows reinforce the more human scale of the entrance: their proportions are people-sized to indicate the human activity inside. Elsewhere domesticity is invoked to moderate the effects of monumentality. The big openings in large walls have glazing cross-bars just like the archetypal doll's house windows. The cross-bar window motif appears high up in the entrance wall, the curved walls, and over the entrances to the Executive.

Architecture mediates between the monumentality of the building and the human scale of users to make it symbolically and functionally legible. Fragmentation of Parliament House into four distinct parts enhances functional legibility, but risks diminishing the symbolic cohesion of the parts. This is allayed by the unifying role of the curved walls, hill, and flag; and by the consistent expression of geometry, structure, architectural elements, materials, and landscaping. The consistency of expression is not achieved through repetition, but through variations on a limited number of themes. This ensures a memorable and intelligible identity for the individual parts as well as for the whole.

The building throughout is distinguished by the structuring intelligence of a coherent and potent architectural idea. This idea is consistently developed and elaborated to engender legibility. The building accomplishes its task as monument, workplace, and urban fulcrum of the National Capital.

As a monument, Parliament House shoulders responsibilities of signification unprecedented in any other Australian building programme. Yet the architectural commitment to making a building of supremely human measure and understanding is beyond question.

What present and future generations make of Parliament House, how the building is received into the national psyche, is not for the architects or for critics to determine. But what may be stated clearly is that everything in the design of Parliament House — from its purely emblematic elements to the never-to-be-seen machinery in the bowels of the building — is the elegant resolution of sustained, purposeful consideration.

Parliament House is the triumphant result of the genius of determination and the cultural clarity of Mitchell/Giurgola & Thorp and their team.

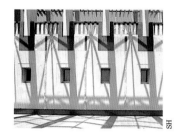

■ *Windows 'punched' through the front entrance wall*

■ *Cross-bar windows in the curved walls*

Romaldo Giurgola

THE ARTS AND CRAFTS OF PARLIAMENT HOUSE

CARL ANDREW

In every civilization of the world for several thousand years, the languages of art and architecture have been spoken in unison — sculpture and painting being as essential to communication as architectural forms and spaces.

Temples in ancient Egypt and Mesopotamia stated the absolute nature of divine power through massive statuary and bas-reliefs as much as through awe-inspiring processional sequences of courtyards, columned halls, and sanctuaries.

Over centuries the gothic cathedral became a skeletal stone structure to support soaring windows which told bible stories in glowing stained glass to a largely illiterate populace. The arched portals were alive with carved saints and visions of heaven and hell.

The baroque movement, with Bernini its greatest exponent, marshalled all its resources — architecture, sculpture, illusionist painting, carving, marquetry, metalwork, gilding, costumes, textiles, and finally music and pageantry — to assert in a complete fusion of architecture and art the glory of the Church Triumphant.

This universal and synergetic relationship between architecture and art was the norm until very recent times. It prevailed in brilliant style through the art nouveau and art deco periods — when architect, painter, and designer were often the one person — and was a theoretical cornerstone of Bauhaus teaching. Walter Gropius wrote that 'Our ultimate goal . . . was the composite but inseparable work of art, the great buildings, in which the old dividing-line between monumental and decorative elements would have disappeared forever'. (*The New Architecture and the Bauhaus*, 1935).

But the period after World War II saw the rise of an aesthetic puritanism among architects which asserted that art could only clutter their design. If it had a place at all, it might take the form of a steel sculpture on a forecourt or a simple tapestry on a foyer wall; the removal of such works would have almost no impact upon the architecture as there was no synergy in their relationship.

Romaldo Giurgola, very much the product of his Italian heritage, was determined that Australia's Parliament House would be rich in works of art in all media and that these would contribute vitally to the philosophical concept of the building and to its functions.

At the earliest stages of designing the building, the architects prepared a major report which specified all the potential locations for works of art and craft and gave notional descriptions of what they might be, with priority ratings and notes on their functional and aesthetic purposes.

This report identified the north-south processional axis — Forecourt, Foyer, Great Hall, Members' Hall, and Main Committee Room — as principal venues for these works, which were to emphasize the architects' concept of this axis as a path symbolizing the transition from past to future.

'This historical sequence is not meant to refer merely to histor-

■ *Michael Nelson Tjakamarra and Pamille Berg discuss his Papunya painting cartoon for the Forecourt mosaic at his home in the Western Desert.*

ical events or periods . . . but rather . . . to the changes in human values which occurred during the slow forging of a complex sense of Australian identity among its people.

'The unique character of the Australian land or continent has been a major, decisive factor in the transformation of those values and hence the qualities of the Australian land form an important and rich source of departure for works of art within that historical sequence of spaces in the building.' (From the brief for marquetry panels.)

At the centre of the Forecourt is a mosaic island of almost 200 square metres set in a ceremonial pool. It signifies Aboriginal habitation in Australia for millennia prior to European settlement.

Aboriginal artists do not work with materials of the durability required for a major work in this location. It was decided to commission a Papunya artist, from the Western Desert region of Australia's centre, to paint a work which would be interpreted as a granite mosaic pavement, the *tesserae* corresponding to the spaced dabs of acrylic paint which have been typical of Papunya painting since the early 1970s. Translation of Aboriginal art into a non-traditional medium is a sensitive issue, and opinions were sought from Aboriginal artists before the project was launched. A mason and an Italian mosaicist were also engaged as technical consultant and fabricator.

Five Papunya artists were invited to submit two design proposals each for the mosaic. The Art Advisory Committee selected a painting by Michael Nelson Tjakamarra which represents gatherings of tribespeople of the dingo, wallaby, and goanna ancestors for important ceremonies. The artist was retained to work with the fabricators of the mosaic to ensure the faithful interpretation of his painting.

(In 1981 the Parliament House Construction Authority had appointed an Art Advisory Committee comprising Romaldo Giurgola and two nominees each from the Australian National Gallery, the Crafts Board, and the Visual Arts Board of the Australia Council under the chairmanship of Sir Laurence Muir, a member of the Parliament House Construction Authority. This committee of arts administrators and practitioners was augmented by parliamentary representatives and it met regularly with the arts programme unit of the architects' office, headed by Pamille Berg, and with the curator of the Parliament Collection, Katrina Rumley.)

Moving inside the building, the first space is the Foyer — symbolically and functionally the place of arrival. The major work here which comprises 20 timber panels with marquetry designs of Australian flora. They are symbolic references to the land, a theme which resonates through all the art works on this public and ceremonial axis.

The concept of panels of inlaid designs of Australian flora and fauna developed from an earlier idea of having the coats of arms of

■ *Foyer marquetry panel depicting the cone — containing edible seeds — of a bunya-bunya tree (Araucaria bidwilli), designed by sculptor Tony Bishop and executed by Michael Retter.*

33

the States and Territories placed between the concrete piers around the Foyer walls. But because coats of arms appear elsewhere throughout the building, it was decided to use the less formal and more decorative flora and fauna elements.

From the designs submitted, sculptor Tony Bishop's proposal was selected. He suggested that the idea of depicting flower, animal, and bird emblems of the States be modified to a freer and more ornamental treatment of plants only, in response to his emerging perception of the decorative demands of the Foyer space. For the north wall he chose to depict the plants used by Aboriginal people before European settlement; then he moved to plants which were important to the colonists, and on the south wall he located some of the plants best known as the floral symbols of Australian States. The development of this work reveals how many of the art works evolved in concept and form with the artists' growing understanding of the philosophy underlying the building.

These panels additionally illustrate how artists and craftspeople have collaborated, often for the first time, with skilled practitioners in other media. In several cases this has opened up new areas of work with exciting potential. Tony Bishop prepared his designs as simple line drawings; their interpretation into the coloured and tonal medium of marquetry was the work of Michael Retter (who had previously worked only as a marquetry hobbyist).

The Foyer contains another work which typifies the architects' concern for refinement of detail and the wish to include, wherever appropriate, the personal and humanizing statement of an artist to temper the powerful formal statement of architectural design.

Two monumental staircases rise on each side of the Foyer, with strongly detailed marble balustrades which inflect outwards at their lower ends. Traditionally the finials might have been marble spheres, but sculptor Anne Ferguson was commissioned to carve four small sculptures in Carrara marble which are classical in character but derive from natural forms and include references to classical drapery. These low-key and personal statements provide unexpected relief to the formal grandeur of this space.

The next major space on the ceremonial axis, the Great Hall, symbolizes the period of European settlement. In contrast to the marble surfaces of the Foyer, the interior of the hall is lined almost entirely with warmly coloured timber panelling. The commanding element here, and the largest art work commission of the project, is a tapestry which covers most of the south wall.

Romaldo Giurgola's recommendation of Arthur Boyd for this commission was based, in part, on his view that this room is the one location where the statement to be made should reflect the maturity which comes from a lifetime of work. Representational content was considered desirable here, a place of high State occasions such as formal banquets and receptions.

■ *The Foyer reception desk designed by Mitchell Giurgola & Thorp.*

■ *Great Hall tapestry designed by Arthur Boyd and executed by the Victorian Tapestry Workshop (detail).*

The work was originally intended as a mural painting but after discussion with the architect it was decided that Boyd would be commissioned to paint a one-quarter sized landscape for consideration; but the concept gradually emerged to use the painting as the design for a tapestry to be woven by the Victorian Tapestry Workshop. This idea grew from the architects' view of this south wall as a screen and Boyd, sharing this view, believed that the visual flatness of tapestry would be more appropriate than the spatial illusionism of painting. (Some of Boyd's earlier paintings had been interpreted as tapestries and he has a long-standing interest in the medium.)

After discussions with Giurgola early in 1983 in London, Boyd painted three large bush landscapes at his property at Shoalhaven and one was selected by the Art Advisory Committee. Although no single landscape can be archetypally Australian, the bush as seen by Arthur Boyd in this painting may, with variation, be found in most parts of the continent.

The architects' intention was that the south wall landscape, devoid of people, identifies this room as an Australian place of past and present, and emphasizes the importance of the land both as generator and conditioner of values which have characterized the country's development.

The first stage of the enormous task of weaving was begun at the Workshop in Melbourne in 1985. Every brush stroke was delineated on plastic film and photographically enlarged to the tapestry scale to provide a cartoon. In view of the extraordinary width of the tapestry — some 20 metres — it was decided to weave it in four sections and to join them. Long-term conservation and handling factors also affected this decision.

The weave density of 2.5 warps/centimetre was selected collaboratively by the Workshop, artist, and architects to enable the unique textural quality of tapestry to be apparent from some distance, and also be appropriate to the vast area of the work.

Technical problems of weaving such large sections were solved by weaving the tapestry with the warp threads running vertically. This enhanced the textural quality of the work by allowing the gently horizontal movements of the bush background to achieve balance with the rugged verticality of tree forms.

Collaboration among the architects, artist, and weavers was continuous. The Director of the Workshop, Sue Walker, often met with Boyd and the architects during the 30 months of weaving. Before commencing work, the entire Workshop staff spent three days in Canberra at briefing sessions with the architects on site to gain understanding of the building.

The tapestry involved up to 14 weavers. A high level of motivation and commitment to the project had to be maintained to ensure the consistent quality of creative interpretation.

One other major art work in the Great Hall, though not as large,

35

involved even more hours of devoted labour in its making. On the eastern wall at the first floor gallery level is a very large-scale embroidery. This gallery is the major public circulation route for views into the Great Hall. It is a highly appropriate space for the embroidery, allowing visual separation from the massive impact of the tapestry, and opportunities for close inspection.

The proposal for this work had been initiated by the Embroiderers' Guilds of Australia in 1980 as a gift to the Parliament for installation in the new Parliament House. The Guilds offered to provide, through their membership in all states, the workforce to embroider a work of monumental size in the historic European tradition of commemorative embroidery.

Such a bold project obviously posed enormous problems of design and co-ordination, and had the potential to be disastrous. The combined efforts of even a small group of embroiderers on a single work would entail problems of common commitment to a design concept and of consistency of interpretation and technique. The involvement in this project of more than 1,000 people across Australia presented formidable challenges indeed.

A brief was prepared by the architects. The work was to be 16 metres long by 65 centimetres high — a shape suited to narrative in the tradition of the Bayeux Tapestry (which interestingly is not a tapestry but an embroidery). It was to be made in eight sections to be allocated to the States and Territories for working by their Guild members. Smaller sub-sections were to be worked separately by country groups.

As with the tapestry, the architects' concept of the Great Hall was that its space, architectural detail, and art works should make reference to the Australian land as the 'conditioner' of European values. In contrast to the monumentality of the tapestry, the embroidery techniques and close focus of the viewer's experience of the work required a more intimate scale for its subject and its treatment.

The Art Advisory Committee selected six artists and designers, who were not all embroiderers but had understanding of textile techniques, to present concept and design proposals. Subsequently the artist/weaver Kay Lawrence was selected to design the work and also to co-ordinate and supervise the production of the embroidery throughout Australia.

In preparation for this undertaking Lawrence embarked upon an intensive three months of reading Australian history. She later wrote that she chose to 'use landscape as a metaphor for the development of European settlement in Australia so that the changes, both sudden and gradual, in the appearance of the land mark the settlers' efforts to come to terms with, and to utilise, their environment'.

There is a rhythmic shift along the length of the design as it moves through the land, settlement, colonization, and development and simultaneously changes from distant views to close-focus details

■ *Great Hall embroidery designed by Kay Lawrence and executed by members of the Embroiderers' Guilds of Australia (detail).*

and from monochrome to colour.

There are references to early records of the landscape as we move from left to right through lyrical countryside, slices of maps and of a Papunya painting, sections of letters, early photographs, botanical studies, and the aftermath of a bushfire, and finish with the sobering image of human habitation in a semi-industrial coastal landscape.

This extraordinarily ambitious project changed the lives of many who participated in it. Several took up serious art studies late in life to develop the creative potential which they had, for the first time, recognized in themselves.

At the centre of the building is the Members' Hall, surrounded by a glazed pyramid through which the giant flag can be seen. The flag and its reflection in the pool below constitute the dominant symbol in the chronological sequence — Australia today.

At the top level of the Members' Hall on the south wall is a major ceramic work by Michael Ramsden and Graham Oldroyd. The design brief required that it should relate to factors in this century which have shaped Australian values, that it should read successfully both as a totality and as fragments from partial views, and that it should exploit the changing light conditions of this space.

Ramsden and Oldroyd chose 'The River' as the overall theme of the work. It runs the length of the wall as a free-form bas-relief and passes through six landscapes which can be read on both physical and symbolic levels.

Through its course the river winds from desert to coast, passing through pastoral and industrial landscapes reflecting the impact of human habitation, on through the natural beauty of rainforest and then through a zone ravaged by bushfire, symbolizing the natural forces of destruction and regeneration. The tiles — modelled, textured, cast, glazed, and fired to achieve a rich range of surface colours, from dry chalkiness to lustred pools of transparent glass — were raw glazed in a very large, specially built kiln at Michael Ramsden's workshop in the Blue Mountains.

Continuing along the ceremonial/chronological axis, the anteroom to the Main Committee Room displays Tom Roberts' very large painting of the first Parliament of Australia, washed by natural light from a conical half dome rooflight above. The hundreds of people portrayed in this painting are contained in a strong tonal composition dominated by the arched curve of the vault of Melbourne's Exhibition Building and a dramatic diagonal stream of light.

These tonal elements were the starting point for Mandy Martin in the early conceptual stages of planning her vast canvas, which covers the upper southern wall of the Main Committee Room — an area of almost 3 by 12 metres.

The architects intended this location for an artwork referring implicitly to the impact of Parliamentary decisions on the future of

■ *Mandy Martin at work on her painting for the Main Committee Room.*

37

Australia. The Art Advisory Committee nominated eight leading painters for commissioned proposals and selected Martin's work as one which had powerful aesthetic qualities and would be compatible with the Parliamentary Committee function of the room.

This was a conspicuous case of the fundamental requirement throughout the building that the character of the work in every location be appropriate to the designated use of the space. In this room members will often endure very lengthy and demanding committee sessions, so the artwork could not dominate in an aggressive or disturbing way.

Although Martin's painting refers to the composition and tonality of the Roberts, it is essentially in marked contrast to it. She has moved away from Roberts' recording of a specific historical event to the timelessness of the land itself. Although it is based on the coastline just west of Adelaide, her landscape has a generic quality; and references to the 19th-century sublime romantic landscape tradition can be read also as an optimistic vision of the future of Australia.

The purpose of Parliament House requires that the authority of the Commonwealth be announced by the coat of arms. The architects' concept of the building necessitates that this traditional emblem be fashioned in new forms to fully engage with the architectural character.

There is an inherent conservatism about coats of arms and a long history internationally of disagreement between officials and artists whenever coats of arms have had to be interpreted as works of art. Recognizing this potential conflict, Stuart Devlin, the London-based Australian silversmith (and designer of Australia's decimal coins), was charged with summarizing the requirements of the Royal Warrant and writing guidelines for the commissioning of the four coats of arms in the building. In each case the brief required freshness of vision.

Six artists were selected to present designs for the major coat of arms on the Great Verandah wall, and Robin Blau — previously known as a silversmith, jeweller, and a sculptor on a small scale — was commissioned.

He grouped the exquisitely worked linear elements of animals and shield into a cohesive whole using stainless steel rod. Its delicate open construction allows it to be viewed from behind the Great Verandah as well as from the Forecourt. Its mirror and satin surfaces glitter in the sunlight and it has a jewel-like elegance atop the massive white marble-clad wall.

Following the success of this work, Blau was asked to design a smaller coat of arms for the Ministerial entrance at the opposite end of the building. This work is also linear and in stainless steel, but in contrast to the angular form of the first, is based on circles and curves.

Gordon Andrews, designer of Australia's 1966 decimal currency

■ *Robin Blau's coat of arms for the Forecourt entrance.*

■ *Mock-up for the Senate coat of arms designed and assembled by Peter Taylor.*

■ *Gordon Andrews' coat of arms for the House of Representatives, executed in bas-relief ceramic panels by the ceramicists Rob and Rhyl Hinwood.*

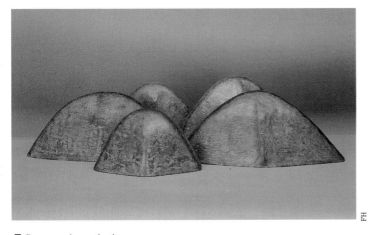

■ *Bronze sculpture for the Executive Courtyard by Marea Gazzard.*

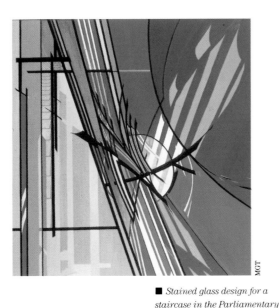

■ *Stained glass design for a staircase in the Parliamentary wings by Cherry Phillips.*

■ *Stained glass design for the Private Dining Room by Klaus Zimmer.*

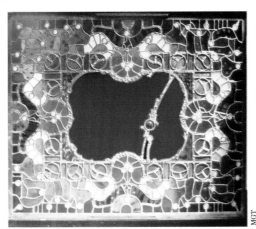

banknotes, was commissioned to design the coat of arms located high above the Speaker's Chair on the eastern wall of the House of Representatives. This work, in bas-relief, is made of ceramic panels cast in raku clay and bisque-fired with a white speckled glaze. The designer collaborated with ceramicists Rob and Rhyl Hinwood, who made the work at their Brisbane studio.

The Tasmanian sculptor Peter Taylor designed and made the coat of arms for the Senate chamber. His work, carved in Tasmanian myrtle, is a free-standing sculpture with glass elements in the shield — a star and bar which entailed collaboration with Anne Dybka and Warren Langley. The coat of arms sits in a cut-out in the timber screen wall, made by Robert Blacklow, which stands behind the President's Chair, echoing the placement of Robin Blau's coat of arms which sits down into the screen wall of the Great Verandah.

Near the southern end of the building's major axis is the Executive Courtyard — an austere, granite-paved rectangular area. From the southern end, a wall fountain splashes down into an indented watercourse which runs along the spine of the pavement and forks through and around a bronze sculptural group by Marea Gazzard.

Gazzard has been well known for decades as one of Australia's leading ceramicists who has occasionally had pieces cast in bronze. Giurgola was impressed by the archetypal landscape references in her organic forms and felt that they would provide an appropriate focus and scale for this space and, with their softly rounded forms and textured surfaces, an appropriate foil to its rectilinear sparseness and grey tonality. The work has direct allusions to the great rock formations of The Olgas but, in a less specific way, evokes landscape elements of more intimate scale which are encountered throughout Australia.

Parliament House has many other art and craft works as well as those commissioned specifically to complement the symbolic, processional, and ceremonial spaces of the building. Symbolically, these may be 'slighter' works, yet they too have significant roles to play in enhancing the location, function, and comfort of the building's working spaces.

At 12 points in the office areas of the Parliamentary wings, the levels of the building are linked by stairwells with metre-wide square and circular windows (for the House of Representatives and Senate respectively). Six artists were commissioned to each provide a pair of flat-glass windows. Very personal statements, diverse in their imagery and symbolism, have been produced by artists Ede Horton, Warren Langley, Cherry Phillips, Mezza Rijsdijk, David Wright, and Klaus Zimmer, using techniques including leading, casting, staining, fusing, and laminating.

Klaus Zimmer also made two larger windows in leaded and stained glass for the east and west walls of the Private Dining Room.

The architects recognized the design and hand fabrication of

39

timber furniture as an important medium in the mainstream of Australian crafts. Indeed, the 20-odd specially designed and handmade furniture types commissioned for the most significant office suites were to be kept *in perpetuum* in Parliament House as part of Australia's collective memory of cultural traditions.

Solid Huon pine panels, some of them moulded and carved, line the office walls of the Prime Minister's suite. The Tasmanian furniture maker and sculptor, Kevin Perkins (who is nationally recognized for his work with that most distinctive and precious of Tasmanian timbers, Huon pine), was asked to design and fabricate the wall panelling with integrated sideboards and display cupboards.

Many important pieces of furniture were designed by the architects for use in the building, for example, the Parliamentary benches in the Senate and House of Representatives chambers and the information counter in the Foyer.

Other special furniture commissions were for individual pieces, such as counters, display cases, tables, chairs and desks.

Glass-maker Maureen Cahill and silversmith Helge Larsen designed and made together a suspended light fitting for the double stair space at the entry to the House of Representatives. Their design is based on associations with the sea as a major influence on the daily lives of most coastal-dwelling Australians.

The fitting is made from elegant vertical steel tubes, curved horizontal steel rods, and suspended glass forms. Its shifting reflections and rhythmic diagonal and spiralling structure recall the constant motion of oceans.

The design for a screen wall behind the reception area of the Parliamentary Library was constrained by high light levels, requiring use of inorganic materials. Warren Langley was commissioned to design and fabricate a mural which shows a grid supporting square slabs of textured and sand-blasted opaque glass, with a relief design based on a map of the Canberra region and incised inscriptions taken from explorers' notes.

The floors of the building, particularly in more intimate spaces, have specially commissioned rugs. Some were designed by the makers and others by painters working collaboratively with weavers.

The rug for the Prime Minister's reception room was designed by the Melbourne painter Lesley Dumbrell, who also designed three rugs for the curved wall circulation area. These designs — involving the play of angular geometric forms and close colour and tonal relationships — enhance the dynamism and activity of this area.

In 1983, in the early stages of construction, the architects proposed an imaginative project to commission photographers from all over Australia to use the building site as the subject matter for personal statements in a series of works.

Harold Cazneaux's photographs of Sydney Harbour bridge and Max Dupain's of the Opera House are among notable earlier examples

■ *Huon pine wall panelling in the Prime Minister's suite designed by Kevin Perkins (model).*

■ *Parliamentary benches, Senate chamber, designed by Mitchell Giurgola & Thorp.*

■ *Parliamentarian's office desk designed by Mitchell Giurgola & Thorp.*

■ *Rug designed by the painter*
Lesley Dumbrell for the curved wall
circulation area.

of non-documentary still photography in this category, but the remarkable body of work produced through this project is unique in Australian photographic history in its scope and diversity.

These photographs were not intended to document the construction of the building (that was done as a separate project by John Gollings). They form part of the Parliament Collection of art works for use in selected public spaces, or to be available for parliamentarians' suites or other office areas.

'The Parliament Collection, comprising some 3,000 works acquired during the construction phase, contributes to the building's unified architectural expression . . . Each of the works purchased, which include paintings, sculpture, and craft objects in various media, was chosen to add to the character and meaning of individual spaces . . . and extend the broadly narrative themes which unfold along the processional and Parliamentary axis of the complex. . .

'The Collection is a highly significant representation of the nations' creative output, principally from the 1980s with important works from earlier periods of Australia's history . . . (It) combines with the program of commissioned works to complete the building's expression of Australian life and culture.' (*Project Parliament*, Number Eight, 1987)

The success or otherwise of the Parliament House art works programme cannot be judged by the extent to which it represents contemporary Australian art and craft. The architects made it clear from the start that the programme would require the most judicious selection of art works, using very specific criteria related to the architectural philosophy of the building and to the particular demands of its character and its spaces. Constraints of location, of size, of character and mood, of subject matter, of durability and accessibility applied to almost every work commissioned or purchased for this building.

Many of Australia's most highly regarded painters, sculptors, and craftspeople are not represented at all. Others are represented by works which might seem less significant in scale than their reputations would lead one to expect. But Parliament House was never intended to be a public gallery of Australian art.

As almost all the art works have been produced during the mid-1980s, it is inevitable that as a collection they will be seen to represent a very specific period in Australian art history. As the building is expected to serve its function for a period of several hundred years, we cannot know how future generations will treat these works. It is possible that some will be replaced in due course, and it is certain that, given the cyclic nature of taste, many will fall into disfavour.

But the preserved documentation of the art programme will clearly prove to future generations that, before Parliament House, no architectural project in Australia had so seriously and systematically introduced and integrated art works of almost every kind into the concept, the structure, and the detailing of a public building.

THE SEMIOTICS OF THE NEW PARLIAMENT HOUSE

IVOR INDYK

The new Parliament House has a clear and unambiguous symbolic duty: it must stand as an expression of the Australian democratic spirit. How is it to fulfil this obligation, given that the spirit it celebrates is itself an emerging entity, open to questioning and self-doubt, at times proud, at others troubled? To this kind of difficulty we should add another, which confronts contemporary architecture as it moves beyond the strictures of modern formalism in attempting to provide richer expressions of cultural value. In relation to the 'stripped aesthetic' of the modern movement, its symbolic gestures may well seem superficial, arbitrary or merely decorative. How, then, does the building resolve these two kinds of difficulty, the one concerning the Australian spirit, the other the means by which it is to be expressed?

At first sight, the pressures seem to have caused the building to fragment. The approaches by road offer a series of partial views, some of which suggest a complex of buildings, while in others one discovers that, contrary to expectation, there appears to be no building at all. This absence is most strongly felt when one stands in what is, after all, the traditional position for viewing a building — directly in front of the new Parliament House, and at a sufficient distance to

take in its salient features at a single glance. Three features stand out: flag-mast, wall, colonnade. The colonnade clearly reads as an entrance, but not to a building so much as to the hill behind. Further, it stands clear of the walls and below them, as if it had been dislocated downwards — between the walls, where one might expect a building, there is emptiness, and the sky. This sense of emptiness is increased by the scale of the flag-mast which, since it is oversized in relation to the colonnade, seems in part at least to be crowning a void. There is an air of incompleteness about the whole scene, as if in the future a town might be expected to grow up behind the walls, and the colonnaded facade rise in a many-tiered palace between them. (This is not as fanciful as it may sound — under 'Symbolism' the competition brief demanded, 'the building must be capable of taking incremental growth'.)

Because it nestles within the hill, critics have likened this 'house' to a tomb, but the symbolism speaks less of the dead than of the about-to-be born, of that which will rise one day from the earth. The colonnade is the sign of an entrance, the walls define the limits of the place, the flag-mast declares *this* place to be of national signifi-

cance — it is as if the basic acts of possession had been performed, the land marked out, so that the process of building might now begin in earnest. The sense of potentiality is further enhanced by the way these features stand out as signs upon the landscape, as if their size in some way guaranteed the reality of the future towards which they gesture.

If Parliament House appears incomplete when seen from close quarters, when it is viewed at a greater distance — across the lake, from the steps of the Australian War Memorial — the situation changes dramatically. Whereas before, Provisional Parliament House had been behind one's back, out of the picture, now it appears as the foundation upon which the new Parliament has been built. Alternatively, we may think of the whole ensemble as a vast palace rising from the lakeshore, its two wings separated by a large internal courtyard. The flag-mast, which had seemed disproportionately large in relation to the facade of the Parliament alone, now forms an appropriate crown to the whole edifice. Furthermore, from this distant perspective the roofs of the two parliamentary chambers emerge from the protection of the previously untenanted walls, their red tiles

announcing the location of the two 'houses' as they glow with colour against the forested slopes of Red Hill behind.

From this standpoint, on the steps of the War Memorial, the Parliament clearly emerges as a unified building, finely proportioned and scaled, its logic and identity clearly expressed. As the Parliament and War Memorial face each other from either end of the sharply defined land axis, it is hardly surprising that the one should assume full significance only in relation to the other. The two are bound by a symbolic reciprocity: the War Memorial stands guard over the ideal of freedom and nationhood represented by the Parliament House, a sombre reminder of the cost of this ideal in terms of human lives, and of the moral qualities required for its defence. Whereas the Parliament House gestures towards the future, the War Memorial tells, with greater certainty, of the heroic past, which it preserves in its exhibitions, in its courtyard galleries lined with the names of the dead, and most solemnly in its Hall of Memory, where the figure of the Australian service man and woman is used repeatedly in allegorical expressions of the spirit of Anzac. This must surely be one of the most determinedly eloquent places in Australia, and here the culture speaks with an unusually confident voice. No surface is left untouched by the signifying impulse, which adorns the walls, the windows, the ceiling, the doors, with an eclectic array of motifs and symbols.

A similar determination is shown by the Parliament House, though its eloquence is necessarily of a different order. The expanse of red gravel which covers the Forecourt clearly represents the desert heart of Australia — at *its* heart, on an island in a ceremonial pool which is meant to symbolize the continent of Australia, there is an Aboriginal mosaic, to represent the history and culture of the first Australians. (This mosaic has striking affinities with the Christian mosaic which lines the cupola of the Hall of Memory, though the one is of the land, the other of the heavens.) At the edge of the Forecourt, where it meets the Great Verandah, the colonnade announces in unmistakably Hellenic tones the advent of European civilization. Then with an abrupt diminution of scale, from the monumental to the domestic, the colonnade gives way to a vine-covered pergola behind, and the connotations are Roman. Inside the Foyer, with another breathtaking transformation, one is transported to the courtyard of an Italian palace of the Renaissance.

The War Memorial conducts it visitors through history, but it is a history of modern warfare, and the qualities it celebrates are essentially martial qualities. As the Parliament is a political house, so its allusions invoke a political history: the intinerary we have just traversed takes us from an indigenous Aboriginal social organization, in harmony with the land, through Greek and Roman democracy, still open to the natural world, to the splendour, the romance, and no doubt the intrigue of the city-states of Renaissance Italy.

But as these associations unfold, so too do their complex implications. Although the mosaic in the Forecourt establishes the primacy of the Aboriginal claim upon the land, this claim is rendered horizontally, in a way which accentuates the towering grandeur of the Western forms which follow. The references to Greece and Rome therefore carry imperial as well as democratic associations; and the siting of the Aboriginal mosaic, before and outside the parliamentary building, may be read as a sign both of primacy, and of exclusion. Similar complexities arise from the insistent references to the Renaissance palace both within and outside the building, and from the hill-city configuration of the parliamentary complex nestling behind its curving walls, again suggesting the Renaissance city-state. The references provide an appropriate expression of cultural achievement and aspiration, but in a parliament they must also suggest, ironically, something of the despotism and civil strife which marked the period.

The eloquence of a building is not a simple matter: it must speak of the bad as well as the good, if it is to command conviction. This applies even more strongly where, as is the case with Parlia-

ment House, what the building speaks about is power. Assertions of authority, pride, achievement, order must seem hollow if not accompanied by some recognition of the contrary ills, of deceit and division, oppression and dispossession. Thus the curved walls which are so dominant a feature of the building operate sometimes as an open embrace, at other times as a barrier. As one walks over the top of the hill and down, the walls seem low in relation to the surrounding landscape, as if beyond them stretched one's own vast estate; but viewed from below, with the empty sky beyond, they invoke the memory of other walls, those which divide and imprison. The Great Hall, well suited by its grand scale for the banquet and the ball, lends itself also to the lying-in-state, and the grand display of grief. In the glass-roofed Members' Hall, at the centre of the building, the paths meet, Senate and Representatives, Executive and Public. The massive portals declare this to be a meeting place, a kind of forum, where the public might mingle openly with its representatives — except that they do not meet, for the public has been channelled onto one level, and the representatives of the public are on another, such is the threat that always attends those who wield power. There is a room that the public may never see, though the power of the people is centred here, and decisions are made which control their lives: this is the Cabinet Room, a room without windows, a box within a box, a bunker isolated from the outside world — here where the power is great, so too is security, and the sense of vulnerability.

Through these and other associations the building extends its discourse of power. In the parliamentary chambers, in contrast to the besieged air of the Cabinet Room, the architecture suggests cool, rational, considered and (one may hope) eloquent debate in a theatrical setting open to the public galleries and the press. In the office wings which serve these chambers, and which are the visible sign of Parliament from the eastern and western approaches, the conception of power is essentially bureaucratic; in the Main Committee Room, with its high cross-barred windows and courtroom procedure, the effect tends towards the inquisitorial. On either side of the parliamentary chambers there are two courtyards, one belonging to the President of the Senate, the other to the Speaker of the House. The one has a colonnade rendered in a style of classical elegance appropriate to the Senate's ceremonial links with royalty; the colonnade in the other, with its corrugated iron roof and timber beams has a verandah-like appearance which speaks directly of the people. It is easy to imagine how these and other features which distinguish the senatorial and the people's houses could become charged with significance in times of political tension. The same may be said of the Executive wing, formed around the Prime Minister's suite and courtyard at the head of the parliamentary complex. The siting has suggested to some a presidential conception of the democratic process, with the Executive standing apart from and possibly even above

Parliament. On the other hand, the regularity with which the ministerial offices are lined up along their corridors suggests the discipline of work rather than the exaltation of power; and while the Prime Minister's suite may be at the head of the parliamentary complex, it is on the bottom of the three floors around the courtyard, astride the entrance, and in this position the Prime Minister plays the role of the *concierge*, the caretaker of the democratic process, rather than its ruler.

A building which courts these associations obviously cannot be ignorant of the complexities of power, and yet this building constantly turns our attention away from the very complexities it raises. So knowing about power in general, it has very little to say about Australian politics in particular. Against its discourse on power it sets another discourse, which speaks of the land as the source from which power springs, and to which those who would wield power must ultimately be accountable. It is in this second discourse that the building speaks of Australia, not as a political entity but as a state of nature, as a land rather than as a nation.

At first sight, it may seem strange that a building which is devoted to the spirit of Australian democracy should have incorporated in its fabric so few references to the Australian democratic tradition, or to the variety of cultural elements which have contributed to the formation of Australian society. There are no allegorical friezes, no state shields, no monumental presentations of the human figure to stand, as in the War Memorial, as the embodiment of the Australian love of liberty and equality. Where emblems do appear, on walls or over entrances for example, they tend to be drawn from an architectural language of geometrical shapes suggestive of balance and order and unity, but apart from their use of the parliamentary colours, without specific social or political reference. The commissioned art works also avoid references of this kind for the most part, preferring instead the language of landscape and natural forms. In fact, the only explicitly political references built into the structure are the Australian coats of arms over the public and Executive entrances and in the Houses of Parliament; and what allows one to think that the effacement of the political is in some measure crucial of the whole idea of the building is the fact that three of these are more or less transparent and the fourth, a bas-relief, so delicately figured as to be almost invisible.

Of course, it is not particularly remarkable that Parliament House, with its essentially political function, should make no reference to the content of Australian politics, for the debates in the Chambers, and the activity around them, may be expected to provide all that is necessary in this respect. Nor is it so strange that this House, which is essentially the house of the Australian people, should have so little to say about the Australian people, with its diverse origins and traditions, for people will come to the building and may

be allowed to speak for themselves. What is significant is that the building should speak so forcefully and insistently of the Australian landscape, as if the spirit of Australia resided here, not in the people or their politics but in the timeless presence of the land.

That this is a building which celebrates the spirit of the land may already be evident on a distant viewing, since it appears to be dug into the hill and the flag-mast crowns the hill rather than a building. That the Forecourt invokes the desert is again appropriate, for the desert is often seen as the most symbolic of our landscapes, the one most highly charged with spiritual significance as representing the heart and soul of Australia. It is in the Foyer, however, that the importance of these references to the landscape really becomes apparent, firstly because although we are now in the building, we still feel ourselves to be outside, such is the force of the allusions to nature, and secondly, because here where the discourse of power reaches something of a climax, it meets and is absorbed into the discourse of the land.

The Foyer is the first of the public rooms in a processional itinerary which includes the Great Hall, the Members' Hall, the two chambers and the Main Committee Room, but whereas in these rooms the role of the public is limited to observation, in the Foyer alone the public is the participant. Here the public gathers, and here in the future, one assumes, the public may seek to express its approbation and its discontent. The Foyer reads as the courtyard to a palace, and its marble staircases and exquisite floor do offer an ennobling experience. But this sense of power is not of a kind to encourage political activity. On the contrary, its effect is one of enchantment, as if one were moving in a dream. No doubt the romance of staircase and balcony contribute to the spell, but what is interesting is the way this Renaissance fantasy gives way to a dream of nature, the green marbled columns and diffused light of the room, in marked contrast to the desert Forecourt outside, suggesting the enchanted world of the forest with its dappled light and shade. This pastoral dream is enhanced by the Australian flora depicted in marquetry panels over the doorways, for although they are ordered in a way that is intended to define three periods in Australian history (Aboriginal, pioneering and contemporary), this allegory is so muted as to be invisible, the overwhelming impression being that of a landscape of forest and flowers, one innocent of any divisions whether historical, social or political.

The subordination of the political to the pastoral is a regular feature of the building, particularly noticeable at the 'hot' points, where paths meet, where there is likely to be action or debate, where decisions are to be taken. In the Great Hall the nation's festivities and solemnities will be performed under the sign of the Land, in this case a wooded hillside looking up towards the sky in the tapestry designed by Arthur Boyd which occupies the whole of the southern wall. On the eastern gallery wall the embroidery designed by Kay Lawrence and executed by the Embroiderers' Guilds of Australia tells of the history of European settlement — one of the few art works in the building to contain specifically historical or social references — but it does so from the land's point of view, and in terms of the changes wrought upon the landscape. In the Members' Hall, at the point where the legislative, public and Executive axes cross — potentially the most political point in the building — a mirror-like pool welling out of stone reflects the clouds passing in the sky overhead. This is perhaps the most telling of all the experiences offered by the new Parliament. At the very centre of Australian political life the political is transcended altogether in a moment which invites an almost mystical communion with nature. It is as if, with its awareness of the consequences of power, the building would have us turn away, as from all human vanities, to contemplate the harmony and the order of the timeless world of nature.

In a similar, though less intense fashion, the colour schemes of the two chambers are shifted from the strong red and green of the Westminster tradition to subdued ochre and grey-green evoking the Australian earth and the foliage of its trees — the coolness of the latter colour in particular inviting detachment from even the most heated quarrels in the House. At the entrance to the Main Committee Room hangs Tom Roberts' 'The Opening of Parliament', a vision of imperial splendour blessed by a heavenly shaft of light; inside, the painting by Mandy Martin which presides over the committee's deliberations borrows the shaft of light, but banishes the assembled multitude, so that it plays instead upon an uninhabited yet portentous coastal seascape. Inside the Cabinet Room, as far as one can imagine from the world of nature, not only because of its location, but also because the political future of the nation will be hammered out here, the deliberations will be conducted under a romantic garland of gum leaves, exquisitely inlaid into panels of silver ash set in the ceiling above. Once again the political is subordinated to the pastoral, the exercise of power to the dream of natural harmony and ease. Outside, in the Prime Minister's Courtyard, the desert heart of Australia returns as an object of contemplation, this time as an expanse of granite broken by a watercourse which flows past a group of bronze sculpted 'hills' aptly called 'The Little Olgas'.

The discourse of nature in the new Parliament House is the result of a collaboration between architecture and the arts and crafts. As in the art works mentioned, the spirit of the land may be invoked directly; but for the most part the discourse works by accumulation, through the range of landscapes it offers — deserts and forests, pastures and wildernesses, mountain, river and sea — as also in its different perspectives and interpretations. As a constant accompaniment to the more dramatic moments, there is the use of natural materials to adorn the surfaces of the building: stone, wool and especially tim-

ber. The latter deserves particular attention, not only for the many different kinds of wood employed — in itself a celebration of the land's resources — but for the fact that the backdrop provided by the timber surfaces is in its own unobtrusive way one of the most eloquent elements in the building. The choice of wood functions as an expression of value: here are Australian hardwoods previously thought unsuitable for joinery; elsewhere, respected timbers are used as signs of supreme value, as in the use of Huon pine in the Prime Minister's suite, the golden timber declaring this to be the highest political office in the land. In the courtyard outside, and in the public terrace over the entrance to the building, the pergolas are made of jarrah rescued from an old warehouse in Fremantle, timber acting here as often in Australia, as a privileged agent of tradition. Implicit in the craftsmanship that has gone into the working of the timber, and the other natural elements, is the expression of a basic ideology, of the dignity of human labour expended upon the products of the earth, of honesty, integrity and individual worth. It may be a heavy burden to place upon the arts and crafts, but the architects would have us see them as the products of a community rooted in the soil, a language formed from the elements of nature, accessible and intelligible to all.

In these ways then, the new Parliament House bears out Giurgola's definition of the relationship between architecture and nature, 'to perform art within nature, by nature, and of nature'. The formula echoes Lincoln's definition of democratic government and the parallel is appropriate. Nature is so strongly and so consistently invoked in this building that we really are required to see the land as the fundamental point of reference for the activities occurring within it, as the source of all power, the foundation of the democratic way of life. There are of course more practical considerations. Giurgola has pointed to the problem architects now face in having to work on an unaccustomed dimension of scale while being attentive to individual human issues: the land underwrites 'an architecture of individual sensitivity within a grand scale', and it seems to have provided a similar frame of reference for the artists as well, confronted with the daunting task of fulfilling commissions of monumental proportions. Then again the land quite literally acts as a common ground upon which the representatives of opposed persuasions might meet: references to the Australian landscape will command unanimity where references of a specifically political or social nature may only produce discord or division.

All of these considerations suggest the same answer to the questions posed at the start of this essay, concerning the difficulties confronted by a building which seeks to express something as elusive as the Australian spirit. The answer, simply put though not simply executed: begin with the land. It is an honest answer, and a humble one, in what is after all the largest, the most expensive, and surely the most enduring of our bicentennial monuments.

JG

PLATES

NEW PARLIAMENT HOUSE CANBERRA

LANDSCAPE PLAN

LDD - P21A

SCALE 1 : 1000

■ *Landscape*

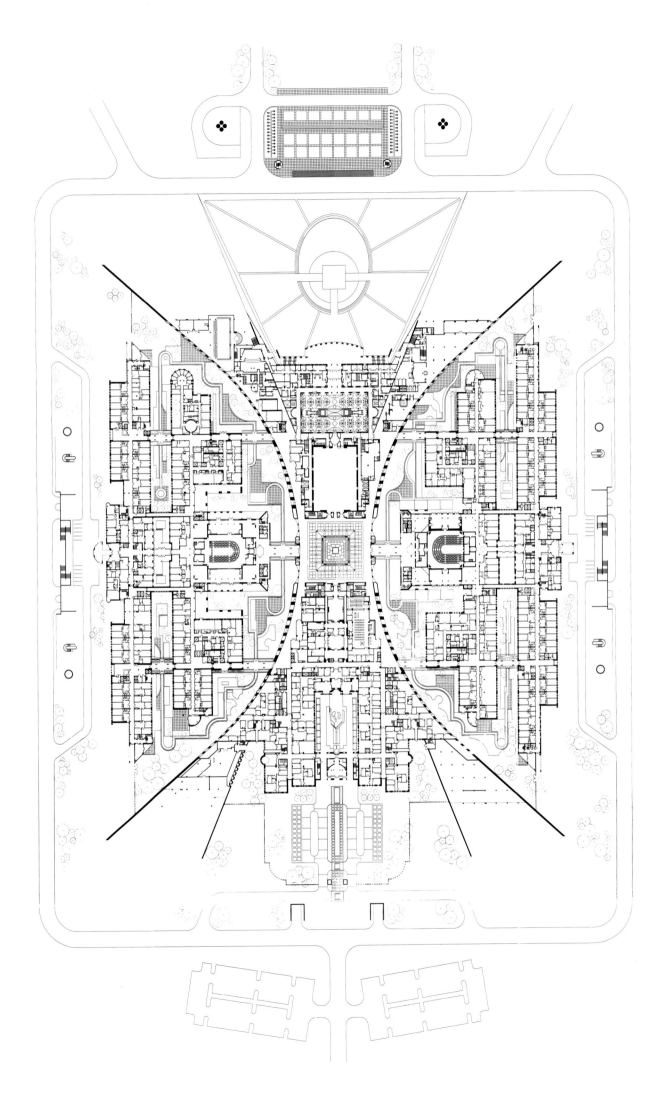

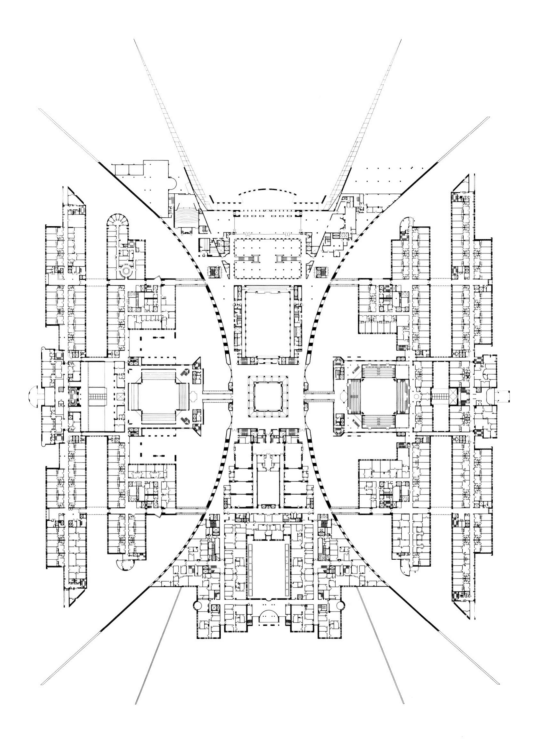

■ *First floor*

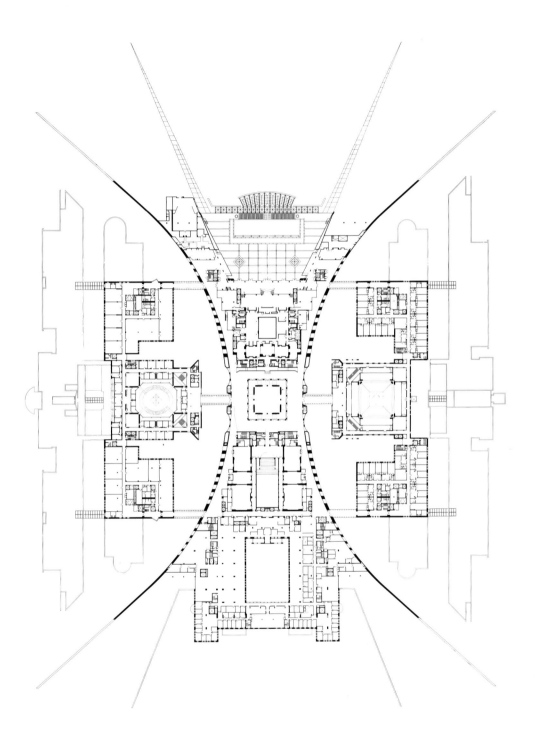

■ *Second floor*

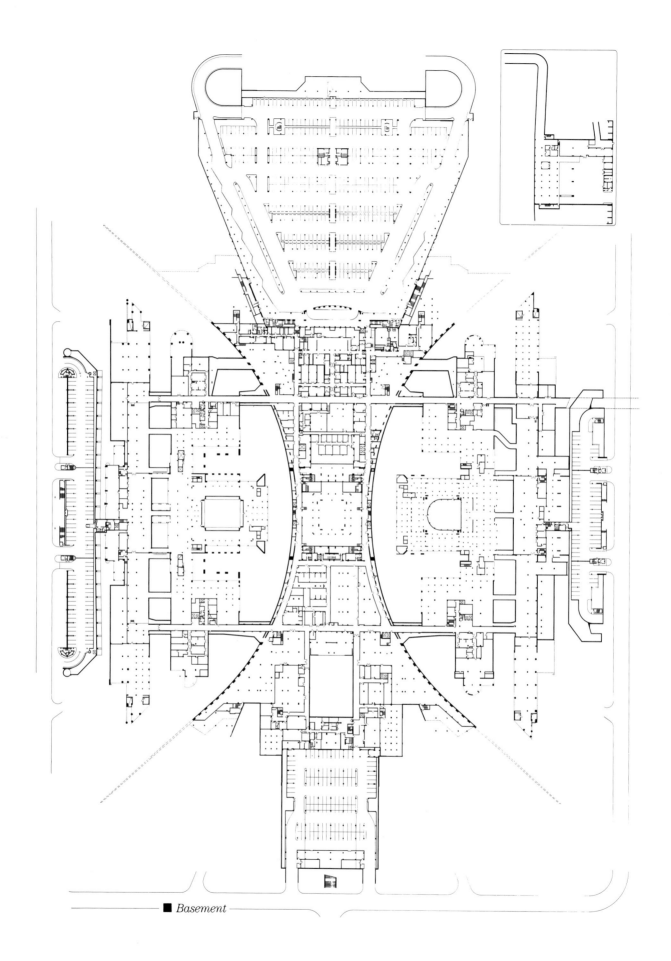

■ *Basement*

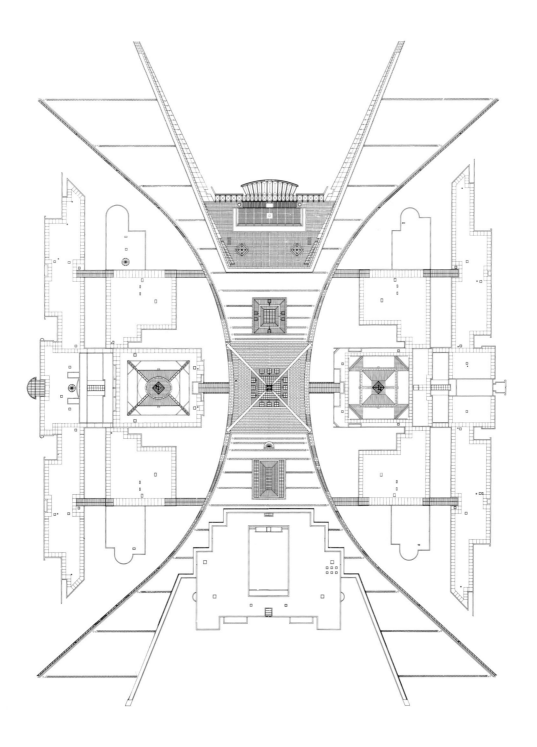

■ *Roof*

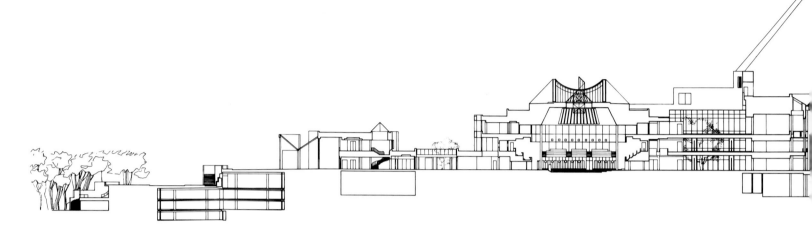

■ *West-east section looking north. From right: House of Representatives porte cochère and entry, Speaker's Courtyard, c*

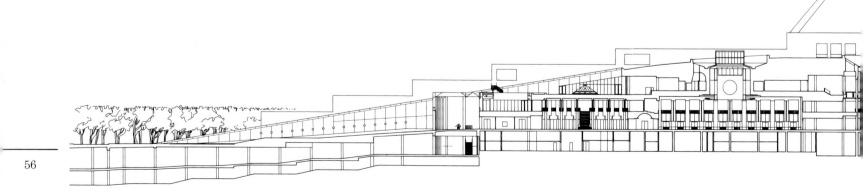

■ *North-south section looking east. From left: Forecourt, Great Verandah, entrance with public verandah and loggia above, Foyer with Members'*
Prime Minister's suite with library above it

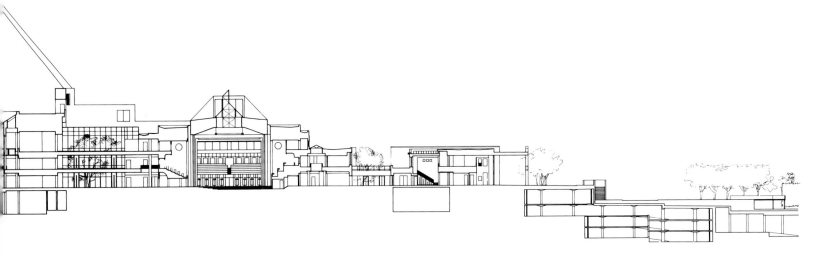

azed link, Members' Hall and flag, glazed link, Senate chamber, President's Courtyard, Senate porte cochère and entry.

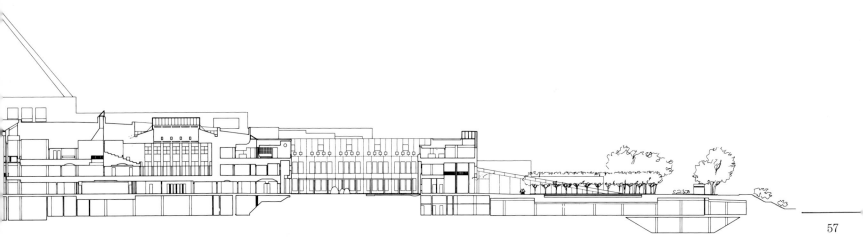

ove, Great Hall with Members' Dining Room and roof monitor above, Members' Hall and flag, Cabinet Room with Main Committee Room above,

or, Executive Courtyard, Executive entrance.

■ *The shape and layout of Parliament House result from simple compositional 'rules'. Each of the four primary functions has its own place on Capital Hill. Two massive curved walls, like a giant X on the landscape, mark the summit of the hill and divide it into four quadrants (fig 1). In the manner of an abstract artwork, three quintessential signs distil the idea 'Australia': the flag, emblem of nationhood; the hill, embodiment of place; and the walls, marks of human inhabitation (fig 2). The hill is reconstructed. To enter Parliament House, the public passes through the portico and into the 'hill' — symbolically entering 'Australia' (fig 3). The Executive building — containing the offices of Prime Minister and Cabinet — is set into the side of Capital Hill, symbolically placed in direct contact with 'Australia' (fig 4). The Constitutional guarantees of independence and freedom of speech in the two Houses are represented by the location of these two buildings standing free of the 'hill' (fig 5). To each side of the two Houses, successive wings seem to have been added (figs 6 to 9). They accommodate the 'business' functions of the Houses and look a lot like office buildings.*

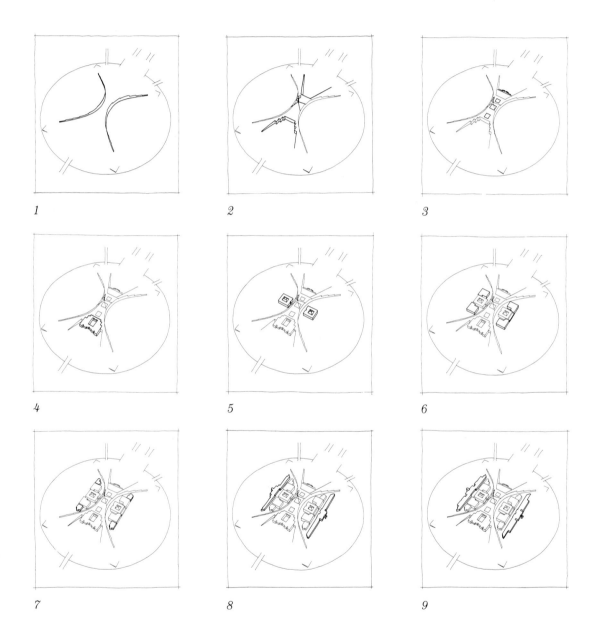

1

2

3

4

5

6

7

8

9

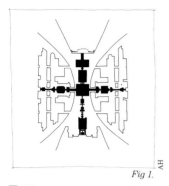

Fig 1.

AH

■ *There are two ways of getting around Parliament House. One is ceremonial and generally symbolic, the other is functional and highly practical.*

The ceremonial paths enter from the four cardinal points and cut right through the building: from north to south, and from east to west (fig 1). They intersect at the symbolic and physical centre of Parliament: under the flag in the Members' Hall. Both routes tell a story. The spaces along the main path (from the north) are arranged as episodes in Australian history. The east-west route has a Constitutional allegory. It is technically possible to pass right through Parliament House along these two ceremonial paths. However, protocol and security demand that they be more symbolic than practical.

Fig 2.

■ *For ordinary use, internal 'streets' criss-cross the building (fig 2). Mapping a way through this grid is surprisingly easy: each corridor ends in light at the edge of the building; each intersection along the way is a place with a distinctive character; shades of green or red identify the east and west sides respectively; specially commissioned art and craft works act as markers; and glimpses of the curved walls, courtyards, Foyer, flag and chambers provide additional reference points.*

■ *Parliament House has two kinds of rooms: those of any large institution: offices, plant rooms, cafeterias; and those where the activity is in the public eye: Foyer, Great Hall, chambers. These spaces are for performances and ceremonies regulated by tradition or protocol. Corridors lead to offices and the like. One suite of rooms is much the same as any other. The public and ceremonial spaces are very different: there are no corridors. With entrances at each end, one room opens into the next, enfilade. On State occasions you can process in a straight line from the Forecourt, through the Foyer and Great Hall, to the Members' Hall. Each ceremonial space has its own character: marble in the Foyer, timber panelling in the Great Hall, white stuccoed portals in the Members' Hall. Yet, like chapters in a book, they are linked by a common thread — the narrative of the processional path. They form a spatial tableau in which each architectural 'figure' acts with the others. Processional routes from the four cardinal entrances are arranged enfilade as spatial tableaux. Each tableau suggests a story: from the north, a history of Australia; the east-west route through the two chambers explains the bicameral basis of the Constitution; the path from the south reveals the role of the Executive.*

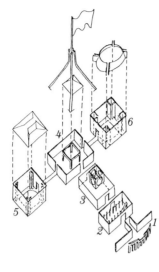

■ Key:
1 Portico
2 Foyer
3 Great Hall
4 Members' Hall
5 House chamber
6 Senate chamber

■ *Members' Hall*

■ *House of Representatives chamber*

■ *Senate chamber*

■ *Great Hall*

■ *Foyer*

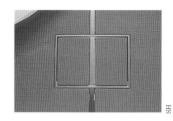

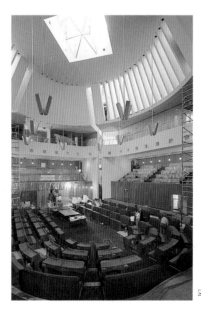

■ *The architects'*
diagrammatic plan
explains the 'colour-cross'
(above), with red hues
for the Senate on the left,
and green for the House of
Representatives on the right.
Their choice of colours was
determined in part by
parliamentary tradition,
but also by the colours of the
Australian bush (top centre).

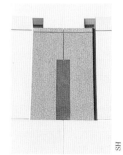

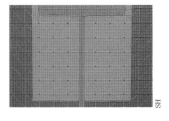

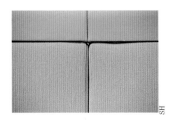

■ *The two chambers in Provisional Parliament House are red (Upper House) and green (Lower House). This tradition, inherited from Westminster, is continued in the chambers of new Parliament House.*

Each chamber is identified by red or green tones in the leather upholstery, carpets, and wall fabrics. Even the timber has been selected for a red or green cast: jarrah in the Senate, and the much lighter grey box in the House of Representatives.

These colours permeate the two Houses: an austere wash of grey-green in the east, and a pale pink flush in the west. Highlights of deep colour come from marble inlays, timber panelling, hand-woven rugs.

There are also geometric distinctions: squares for the Lower House, circles for the Upper. The Senate porte cochère is semicircular and clad in red marbles; its opposite number, for the House of Representatives, is green and cubic. Inside, the angular, prismatic geometry in the east is counterposed by the voluptuous curve of the Senate stairs and elliptical form of the chamber ceiling. Though very similar in layout, the use of colour and geometry makes it impossible to confuse the two sides of Parliament.

65

■ *Parliament House has four front doors, one for each 'building' in the ensemble. Each is different and offers clues about the spaces inside.*

The two Houses are heralded by portes cochères, architectural forms which signal arrival by vehicle and have the necessary public quality for entrances used by hundreds of parliamentarians.

In addition to the way they signal arrival and entry, the portes cochères also act as billboards for the Houses. Seen from the boulevards encircling Parliament House, they are highway-scaled 'signs' embellishing the otherwise utilitarian facades of the parliamentary office wings.

The Senate porte cochère, with its red marble and circular geometry, has a lavish architectural treatment that reflects the sumptuous character of the Upper House in relation to the Lower House.

Its transparent glazed roof, reminiscent of the ceremonial front entry portico, contrasts with the simply plastered solid soffit over the House of Representatives porte cochère. Such play-offs are sustained in the green marble inlays and square geometric motifs, which state themes continued inside throughout the House.

67

■ *In the working quarters of Parliament House, the staircases have identity tags. They are stained glass windows — one for each of 12 stairwells in the office wings of the House of Representatives and Senate. Deliberately vivid, these act as place signs for parliamentarians and staff in the building's complex grid of corridors. Their luminosity and rich colours are intended to be cheerfully uplifting and individually memorable (as well as lighting the tops of the stairwells).*

The windows are round (approximately 1m in diameter) in the House wing, and square (approximately 1.1m) in the Senate area (a twist employed repeatedly by the architects to help identify similar places on opposite sides of the buildings). Commissioned artists were Warren Langley and Cherry Phillips (NSW), Ede Horton, David Wright and Klaus Zimmer (Victoria), and Mezza Rijsdijk (ACT). All were briefed to prepare strong designs based on subjects which would not conflict with the building's dual role as workplace and national symbol.

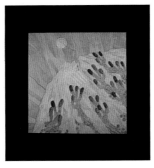

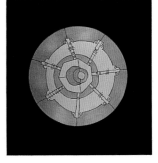

■ *Some cartoons prepared by stained glass artists for windows lighting stairwells in the Parliamentary wings. Clockwise, from top right: Ede Horton, Klaus Zimmer, Warren Langley, Ede Horton, Klaus Zimmer, David Wright.*

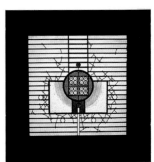

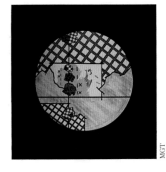

On this page is one of two stained glass windows Klaus Zimmer produced for private dining rooms in the Executive wing. His cartoons for the leading and colours are shown (top), the finished work (centre), and a detail (bottom).

■ *In 1911 an international competition was held to plan Canberra. The winning design — by Chicago architect Walter Burley Griffin — blended architecture and city planning in an organic relationship with the landscape.*

Griffin used natural topography — the hills and Molonglo River valley — as the starting point. The valley was flooded to form a lake. The ceremonial spine for the new city was a line drawn from Mount Ainslie across the lake to the knoll he named Capital Hill. Along Griffin's 'Land Axis', a war memorial and parliament building were located. Radiating from the top of Capital Hill, two avenues formed the sides of the Parliamentary Triangle, with the lake at its base. At the ends of the Land Axis — on top of Mount Ainslie or under the flag above Parliament House — Griffin's orchestration of city planning and natural landscape into a single majestic composition is clearly seen.

The curved walls amplify this urban vision by extending the sides of the Parliamentary Triangle to form an apex and focusing the Land Axis on the flag. Parliament House is seen at the centre of the surrounding countryside, at the centre of Capital Hill, and symbolically at the nation's centre.

■ *The Forecourt may be thought of as an outdoor room, walled on three sides. It is the first of a series of rooms along the ceremonial route into Parliament House. This route actually begins on the far side of Lake Burley Griffin at the War Memorial. The Memorial (symbolizing patriotism) and Parliament House (nationhood) are visually connected by the Land Axis. Across the city these two buildings are locked into a symbolic dialogue about 'Australianness'. With its sunburnt gravel floor, sloping sandstone-coloured sides, and central pool, the Forecourt is reminiscent of deserts and billabongs — of Australia's much mythologized red*

centre. The idea of an
Aboriginal place as the
setting for Parliament House
is introduced in the large
mosaic at the centre of the
pool: a Papunya ground
painting depicting the
gathering of clans.
The sense of the Forecourt as
a gathering place is
emphasized by the embrace
of the angled side walls.
The portico — with its white
marbled cladding, square-cut
form, and three simple
openings at the centre
surmounted by the coat of
arms — is unmistakably
like the familiar front
of Provisional Parliament
House. Memories of the
old building are retained
in the new.

■ *Beneath the Forecourt stretches an enormous car park for visitors to Parliament House. Suspended above this massive excavation is a reinforced concrete floor which has been formed over a system of waffle pans (left) that reduces the mass of concrete without sacrificing strength.*

Canberra has a climate of extremes — producing an annual temperature range of over 40°C. The grassed slopes of Capital Hill protect the central ceremonial spaces inside Parliament House, but the exposed northern Forecourt receives the full effects of the heat and the cold. With changes in temperature, the expansion and contraction of the Forecourt's concrete floor is taken up by flexible 'expansion' joints. They are camouflaged as a radiating pattern of granite paving that regulates the Forecourt's expanse of red gravel set in bitumen. (The red here makes a visual connection with the red gravel on Anzac Parade, linking the War Memorial, Parliament House, and Griffin's Land Axis as an urban piece.) At the entrance to Parliament House is the Great Verandah. Its outer edge is a screen wall: a colonnade of giant concrete columns (left) clad with matched and polished marble panels.

■ *The Forecourt nearing completion: its structural carcase in place, and only the finishing touches of fine surface materials still to come. At the centre is the elliptical form of the pool with its square of paving awaiting the Papunya mosaic.*

■ The design of the Forecourt mosaic represents a central meeting place for all races and cultures. The Forecourt celebrates Australia's earliest settlers, so it is appropriate that an Aboriginal artist, Michael Nelson Tjakamarra, was asked to create the centrepiece. His design, submitted as a painting at one-tenth scale, was selected from the invited submissions of five artists from the Papunya desert settlement north of Alice Springs. With distinctive pointillist strokes reminiscent of his tribe's traditional sand paintings, Tjakamarra's design shows the tracks of different native animals (in white). They are the signs for different clans of Papunya people. The mosaic represents diverse groups moving towards Canberra depicted as circles at the centre of the composition.

Stonemasons Aldo Rossi, Franco Colussi and William McIntosh recreated the design as a 14m square mosaic of more than 70,000 individually shaped stones cut from granite of seven colours.

The pattern of circles and squares formed by the mosaic and its encircling pool echoes the geometric theme of Parliament House (a square building set in a circle of bush). The radial sides of the Parliamentary Triangle are reflected in the radial tracks in the mosaic.

■ The Forecourt mosaic reinforces symbolic connections between Parliament House and the War Memorial: the radial pattern of the mosaic inside the dome of the shrine (representing spirits of the war dead) rises to a central circle (heaven). Though the cosmologies differ, both mosaics share similar allegorical themes.

■ *The transparency is a surprise. The coat of arms created by Sydney silversmith Robin Blau for the Forecourt entrance to Parliament House has all the drama and heraldic significance of a traditional coat of arms. Yet — like the image of Parliament House itself — the authority and majesty are not expressed forcefully. Stainless steel was chosen because it would not stain adjacent marble finishes, and the tracery of tube linkages allows the coat of arms to be read from the public terrace behind. Thousands of welds join the tubes to form the finished piece, which measures approximately 4 × 4.5m. Based loosely on Aboriginal 'X-ray' drawings, it acknowledges the dedication of the Forecourt to Australia's native inhabitants. Repetitive sequences of triangles echo the geometry of the flag-mast and glass roof of the Great Verandah. On the shield between the rampant emu and kangaroo are the emblems of the six States of Australia. Robin Blau has also designed and made the coat of arms for the Executive building. It is similar in style and construction but, following the architecture's play of circles and squares, is contrastingly curvilinear.*

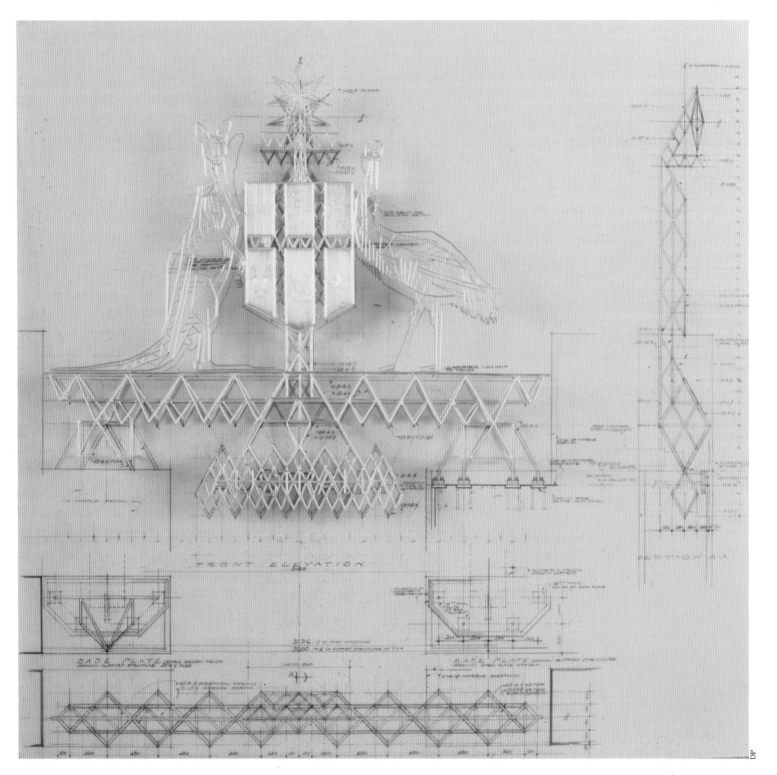

■ *Demonstrating the professionalism and technical skill
demanded for the craft works in Parliament House are this working
drawing and sterling silver scale model prepared by Robin Blau for
the principal coat of arms over the Forecourt entrance.*

■ *Behind the marbled portico (top) that 'remembers' the front of Provisional Parliament House is a glazed 'verandah' which is overlooked from a loggia along the first floor public terrace (top right). Developing the entrance design required sketches such as this early study for the front doorway (bottom right), models, and drawings detailing the full expanse of the inner entry facade (centre).*

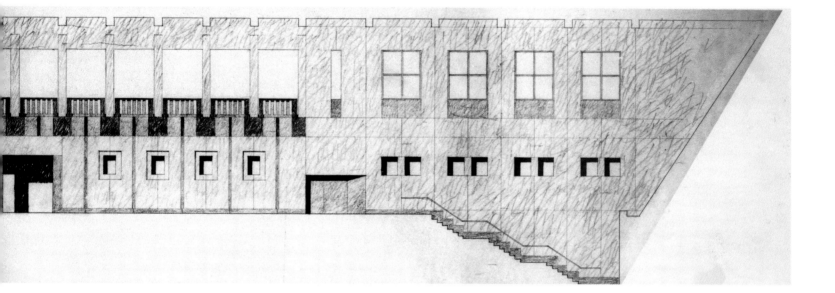

■ *Above: between the portico and the doorway into Parliament House there is a significant shift in scale from monumental to human dimensions.*
Left: using coloured water to test the Forecourt pool for leaks.

THE GREAT VERANDAH

■ *The Great Verandah is the public face of Parliament House, front door and also backdrop for ceremonies in the Forecourt. Its design reflects the architecture of Provisional Parliament House: the new building remembers the old in the shared form of their porticoes.*

The Great Verandah's screen wall presents a simple trabeated structure of columns and beams. The two sides of the portico remain straight, while the centre section swells forward in an architectural gesture of welcome.

The portico structure is reinforced concrete clad with slabs of white Carrara marble just 40mm thick. The marble was selected for its grain while it was still in the ground by the architects at the quarry face (top left). To best present the effect of the grain, each cladding slab is a thin veneer sliced from a single block of stone. It is made obvious that the columns are not solid marble: the joints are left open instead of being filled with mortar as conventional load-bearing masonry dictates.

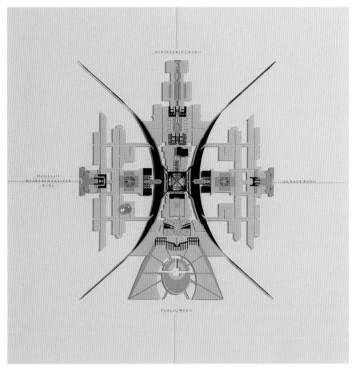

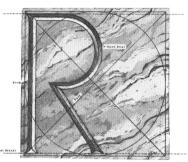

■ *A comprehensive system of signs, including a custom-designed alphabet, has been developed by Emery Vincent Associates for Parliament House. With upwards of 4,000 rooms, the 3,500 workers and estimated 5,000 visitors each day need guidance around the building.*

A style of lettering was required which could be carved in stone, screenprinted onto timber and glass, cast in metal, inlaid, or etched. This ruled out typefaces without serifs: the short flourishes, dating from Roman times, are a necessary part of the technique of chiselling letters in stone.

Letters without serifs (sans-serif), such as the modern Univers — because they are highly legible — have become synonymous with airports, railway stations, and hospitals. The symbolic and ceremonial character of Parliament House demanded a more classical and less utilitarian letterform. Traditional Roman-style letters — though practical — were anachronistic in a new building characterizing Australia.

After studying colonial Australian letterforms based on classical alphabets — as well as ancient Roman examples — Emery Vincent Associates specially designed a versatile serif face crafted from classical principles of geometry and based on Australian precedents.

■ *Many internal direction signs are supplemented by an abstracted three-dimensional map of the building. On it, key architectural features are incorporated as reminders of important rooms and spaces.*

Apex: Pointed

Stem: Left

Stem: Right Hand

Foot Ser

93

■ *Two requirements draw Parliament House in different directions: its significance as a publicly accessible monument, and its purpose as a work place for thousands engaged in the business of government. The conflict has been resolved partly by dividing Parliament House into separate zones, with offices to each side of a central ceremonial route. Public access along this route is necessarily restricted, because the ceremonial spaces – particularly the two chambers – are also work places.*

In the Forecourt and Foyer, people move about freely. But beyond here they become observers only and access is channelled and limited. On the first floor level at the front of the building is the public terrace. Here, confronting the majestic vista of Griffin's Land Axis, the public may stroll in the sunshine and under a loggia covered with wisteria. The loggia – built from jarrah rescued from a demolished woolshed in Fremantle – provides an intimate human scale at the transition point between the monumental space of the Forecourt and passage into the building. Significantly, the public enjoy the building's finest views.

The visual, aural, and tactile impressions of the Forecourt are quite unlike those inside the Foyer. Hot reddish browns are relieved inside by cool greenish greys. Dazzling sunlight is turned into gently filtered toplighting. Rough exterior textures of precast concrete and gravel contrast with smooth interior surfaces of finely finished marbles and timbers; the crunch of gravel underfoot is transformed to the slippery silence of polished marble. The Forecourt is an empty expanse; the Foyer is crowded with columns. The scale inside shifts from being urban and monumental to more architectural and measurably human. Outside, the approach to Parliament House presents the visitor with isolated architectonic elements: the amphitheatre form of the Forecourt, an open screen wall at one end, and curved walls stepping up the slopes of Capital Hill to the flag. Parliament House is sensed not so much as building but as place — a gathering place, under Capital Hill, beneath the flag. Only on entering the Foyer, with its familiar features of doors, windows, stairs, vertical walls, does Parliament House become a 'building'. Perceptions have been subliminally heightened to make the drama of arrival memorable.

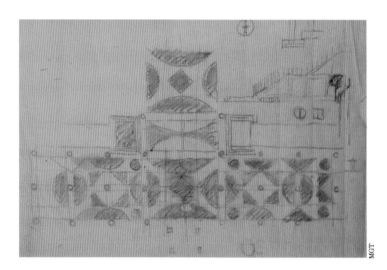

■ *The sense of arrival experienced in the Foyer has a symbolic dimension. Whereas the Forecourt expresses an 'outback', 'Aboriginal' atmosphere, in the Foyer there are powerful evocations of old Europe. The gleaming marble floor looks Roman (its geometric design is very similar to the distinctive paving of circles and squares in the Pantheon). The stairs look familiar too, being modelled on one of Europe's most famous grand staircases — in the Doge's Palace, Venice. The inlays of marble on the sides of the stairs might be abstracted from the walls of the Duomo in Florence.*

The architectural signals are not entirely European. Marble cladding the forest of columns is the grey-green of gum tree trunks; an exquisite marquetry frieze of native plants encircles the room. The architectural features give added significance to the traditional function of the Foyer as space of arrival. Function and embellishment unite to create a metaphor for the arrival of Europeans in Australia.

The symbolism of the Forecourt and the Foyer contributes to the cultural myth of Australianness. The contrasting architectural treatments ('Aboriginal' outside, 'European' inside) reflect the essential dichotomy of Australia as a people.

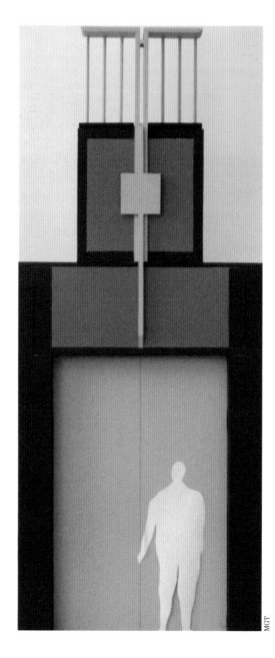

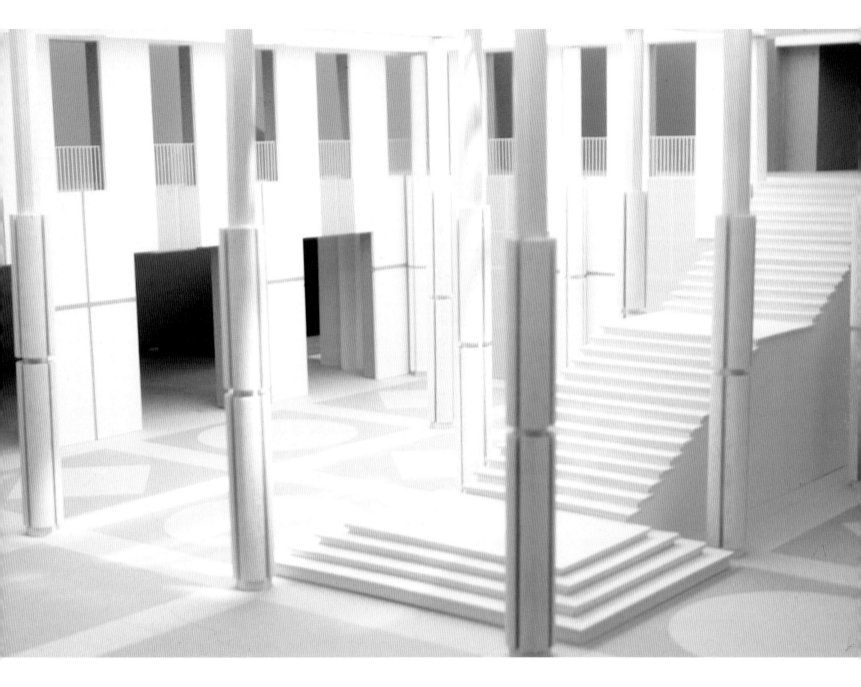

■ *Most details were subjected to an exhaustive process of*
comparing alternatives and testing promising solutions in model
form. These ranged from crude rough renderings (top left),
to mock-ups exact in every detail (left), to finely detailed models
portraying spatial and lighting effects (above).

■ *Twenty panels of timber marquetry contribute to the complex imagery of the Foyer. Each panel illustrates a significant native plant. They emphasize the Foyer's symbolic references to the arrival of European explorers and settlers, and enhance visual allusions to a gum tree forest suggested in the timber wall panelling and green-grey marble column 'trunks'.*
Six species of native flora important to Aboriginal people as food sources are represented above the northern entrance doors leading from the Forecourt (a subtle reminder of the Aboriginal associations of the Forecourt). On the opposite side of the Foyer, above doors into the Great Hall, six species characteristic of Australia are depicted. These include a eucalypt, the wattle, and several banksias noted in the diaries of botanist Sir Joseph Banks in 1770. Eight more species — including casuarina, the tree used as Australia's first flagpole — are shown on the eastern and western walls.
The marquetries were designed by Adelaide artist Tony Bishop and were made in Sydney by Michael Retter. They are approximately 1.3m square, executed on a base veneer of coachwood with jarrah borders. Up to 12 other timbers were used in each design.

■ *Tony Bishop and Michael Retter collaborated on two other marquetry projects for Parliament House: a frieze of eucalypts for the Cabinet waiting room; and a 6.5×2m panel for the Cabinet Room ceiling (centre right). This highly realistic depiction of eucalypts comes complete with Tony Bishop's humorous inclusion of tiny blowflies, cicadas, dragonflies and other 'bugs' that have evaded the sophisticated security measures taken to eliminate electronic versions.*

BF

BF

BF

BF

JG

BF

BF

■ Across the Foyer two monumental staircases face each other. They are concrete, finished with white Carrara marble and geometric inlays of 'granitello nero' and 'atlantide rosa' marbles. The same materials form the floor pattern, also derived from squares and circles to underline the highly geometric character of the building.
The entire Foyer is designed around a grid of squares. This is picked up in the floor pattern and reflected in the ceiling of fibrous plaster trimmed with white birch. A forest of 48 octagonal columns reduces the room's monumental proportions to a more human scale, creating ideal assembly points for small groups of people. The columns are clad with circular sleeves of green/grey 'cippolino' marble broken by bands of dusty pink 'atlantide rosa'
Above the marble sleeves, the columns are finished with a more prosaic coating of plaster which reveals their octagonal profiles. With this device the ceiling appears to float above the Foyer, lighting the upper reaches of the space. It also has another purpose: to disclose the columns (and the entire building) as an assembly of elegant veneers concealing rough concrete base-structures.

■ *By November 1982 the Foyer's forest of columns was in place (top left). Two years later, with the base-structure complete (top right), the veneer of marble finishes could proceed (centre left). The architects made many study sketches for the column sleeves and stair balustrades (bottom left).*

■ *The central concept of the Constitution — that Parliament is the people — is symbolized in the Foyer. This is the primary public space within the building — the 'people's place' (in the same way as the chambers might be considered to 'belong' to parliamentarians). As the public's room, the Foyer is the most luxuriously appointed space in Parliament House. Rich polished marbles and timber marquetry offer a sumptuous contrast to the much simpler materials of the chambers.*

A foyer marks the point of arrival in a building. First impressions are important and foyers are often decorated

with expensive materials such as marble. The many columns would get in the way of most ceremonial activities, but here they organize the processional route and make the Foyer a fine gathering place. Individuals can cluster in small groups against the columns, unlike the monumental open space of the Forecourt, where people assemble as a crowd. The Foyer space has a more human dimension. Grandness of space, splendour of materials, and sense of high craftsmanship reveal the Foyer as the ceremonial entry and a breathtakingly beautiful meeting place for the public.

■ *Before excavation*

■ *18th September 1981*

■ *2nd October 1984*

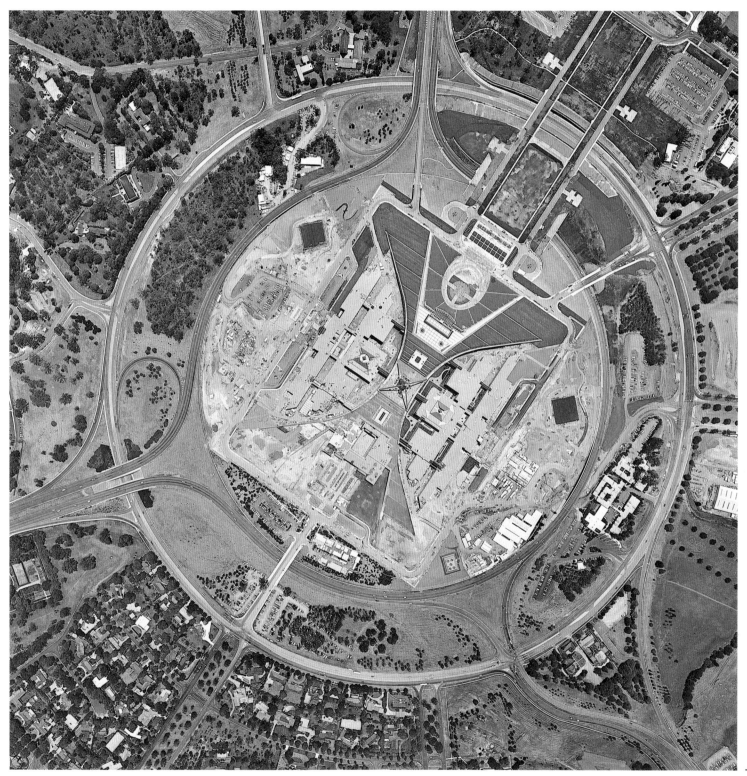

■ *11th December 1987*

■ *The basement keeps Parliament House alive. All the building's functions are controlled there by a sophisticated life support system with some similarities to the human body. Breathing begins in a basement air conditioning room linked by ducting to a network of smaller plant rooms on higher floors. These control air temperature, movement, purity and sometimes humidity in different areas. Sustenance comes from basement kitchens separately equipped to prepare foods as various as fish, pasta, bread, pastries and sauces. They are linked by lifts to general kitchens, including those serving the Great Hall, cafeterias, dining rooms and the suites of senior parliamentarians. An extensive cellar stores all liquid refreshments; some can be piped 'on tap' to bars around the building. A complex nerve system also stems from the basement, which houses many electrical, electronic, computer, communication, sound and vision, security and fire prevention systems. There is a document transfer system of tracks and carriages mounted on the basement ceiling; it will be used when several signatures are required on important papers. The basement's other facilities include extensive car and bus parking, furniture repair workshops, many storage and maintenance rooms, a small police station, two printeries, a telephone exchange, emergency electricity generators, dining and locker rooms for service staff and an internal 'road' system for deliveries and waste removal by forklift trucks.*

■ *There are places for parliamentarians to relax as well as work. Almost encircling Parliament House is a small bush-like park of local gums. Paths meander through it leading to tennis courts set in glades. On the car park roof in front of the entrance to the House of Representatives, a parterre garden is being established. Inside the building there are billiards rooms next to the Members' Private Dining Room, and on the ground floor, under the grassed north-east ramp, a swimming pool (right).*

■ *The ceaseless recording of parliamentary proceedings is undertaken by Hansard's stenographers. Working in relays, each takes a place in a chamber for a few minutes at a time, then returns to small rooms in Hansard's offices at the northern tip of one of the Senatorial office wings. There the notes are transcribed and sent to the basement printeries to become Hansard entries. Parliament's proceedings generate a prodigious amount of data which is housed in the Parliamentary Library on the top floor of the Executive building — haunt of research assistants. On the ground floor of the Executive is the Media Library (top and bottom), with magazines and newspapers close at hand to the chambers for parliamentarians' ready reference.*

■ *Floors were not forgotten in the art and craft programme of works commissioned for Parliament House: 13 rugs were handwoven for selected corridors, waiting areas and the Parliamentary Library reading room. The designs, by seven artists from several disciplines, are decorative abstracts, of which two have obvious Australian connotations (see Jenny Kee's design, far right, with its collection of native flowers — waratahs, flannel flowers, Sturt's desert pea — and Aboriginal motifs).*

All the rugs (apart from one designed and made by Sydney weaver Lise Cruickshank) were woven by Liz Nettleton and her team of five. They are flatwoven (in the manner of Oriental khelims), using commercial carpet wool as the weft and high-twist cotton twine as the warp. On this page (right) is Nola Jones' rug in its three stages of production: the designer's cartoon (top), being fabricated in Liz Nettleton's workshop (bottom), and the finished work (centre).

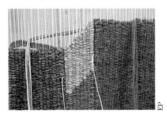

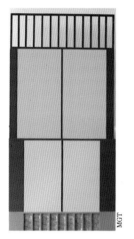

■ *In the 'room of the land', timber is the main finish. The Great Hall floor is herringbone parquetry of West Australian jarrah (laid on plywood and neoprene foundations developed for gymnasiums to give the floor the necessary spring to function as a ballroom). The floor pattern is intersected by strip inlays of blackbutt (on the north-south axis) and ebony (east-west). These form a grid which helps modulate the monumental scale of the room, leading the eye to the Arthur Boyd tapestry on the southern wall. (The grid also assists function organizers arrange tables and chairs.) In the centre of the floor, blackbutt inlays form a geometric motif which alludes to Australia's six States. Between the rhythmic sequences of columns along the side walls are panels of white birch veneer contrasted by edgings of darker timbers: brush box and ebony. Balustrades to the galleries are brush box. To develop the design for the wall panelling, the architects first prepared study sketches before making small-scale mock-ups that accurately represented the final colours and materials (above).*

■ *The Great Hall is the dining room of Parliament House. When the Government entertains, it's on a grand scale: 800 people sit down to a silver service dinner, 1,500 turn up for cocktails.*

Even empty, the pomp and splendour of this room can be sensed. At the far end, under the tapestry interpreting Arthur Boyd's painting, stands the Great Table. Although the room is enormous, it is also familiar. White columns and the central skylight echo the main reception space of Provisional Parliament House, King's Hall. Parquet and timber panelling evoke the ambience of a Federation period dining room.

The colonnade of columns marching down the side walls pace out the length of the Great Hall. The door-sized wall panelling gives the room a human measure. Contrasting colours of timber panelling between the columns define the head-and-shoulders motif in the Foyer and the entrance doorway. Behind the columns are the public galleries, faced with brushbox balustrades similar to those found in the Foyer. (On the public terrace overlooking the entrance, this balustrade detail occurs again, but executed in red marble.) Entrance, Foyer, and Great Hall are members of the same architectural 'family'.

■ The Great Hall tapestry is the 'magnetizing focal point' of the room. Its subject — a dense forest of eucalypts on a hillside — is appropriate to the symbolic image of this 'room of the land' and complements native timbers in the panelling and parquetry flooring.

The tapestry — 20m long and 9m high — interprets a painted cartoon by Arthur Boyd. His compelling vision of the landscape captures the Australian spirit of place. A team of artist-weavers spent three years making the tapestry on four massive looms at the Victorian Tapestry Workshop. To enhance the design of tall trees, the work has been woven upwards, with the warp threads vertical.

At the top of the tapestry, above the ridge line, blue skylight shines through the trees. It is a powerful evocation of Ben Chifley's 'Light on the hill' address to the Australian Labor Party in 1949: 'We have a great objective — the light on the hill — which we aim to reach by working for the betterment of mankind not only here but anywhere we may give a helping hand.'

Seen from below, the blue sky becomes the focal point, compelling the gaze upwards to take in and connect the symbolism of the Great Hall, tapestry, and the flag on top of Capital Hill.

■ Initially the architects envisaged a painting which could symbolize this space as the 'room of the land'. Arthur Boyd (seen here, top, working on the painting) proposed instead a tapestry interpreting his work. The Victorian Tapestry Workshop selected yarns (left) that matched precisely the colours in Boyd's cartoon (centre).

VTW

■ The architectural vision of Parliament's Great Hall as a 'room of the land' is underscored by two major artworks which hang there. One is a woven tapestry, the other an embroidered panel. Both are the result of close collaborations between the architects, Australian artists, and teams of accomplished craft specialists (one professional and one amateur). Although the images are different, both works study a single theme: the influence of the land on Australia's development as a nation and its impact on the social values of inhabitants.

■ *A work reminiscent of the Bayeux Tapestry has been commissioned for Parliament House. The 16m-long embroidered panel narrates the history of Australians' involvement with the land. Mounted along the east wall of the public gallery in the Great Hall, the design by Adelaide artist Kay Lawrence was executed by over 1,000 members of embroiderers' guilds throughout Australia, who donated their expertise as a Bicentennial gift to the nation.*

The linen base cloth is worked with a variety of appliqué and embroidery techniques, using cotton, linen, wool, and some synthetic fibres. Some of the appliqué fabrics are scraps from colonial and Victorian patchwork quilts. Sophisticated conservation techniques have been used to stabilize the colours and intricate embroidery. The design shows how the peculiarities of the Australian continent — its harsh land and climate — helped mould a unique national character from the British traditions of early settlers.

Each of the panel's eight sections deals with a different period, from before European settlement to Federation in 1901. Some of the 33 pictorial images are based on early maps and prints. Several have accompanying inscriptions taken from Australian prose and poetry.

■ *Kay Lawrence's cartoon (above) for the Great Hall embroidery. Members of embroidery guilds gathered all over Australia to work on small sections which were then pieced together. In a narrative that begins with the bush, it tells the story of European settlement of the land. Maps, old photographs and documents, along with Lawrence's drawings, are all exquisitely rendered with needle and thread (right).*

■ *The Great Hall,
Parliament's reception
room, is a flexible venue for
parties, a grand place for
State occasions. In contrast
to the Foyer, the space is
clear and uninterrupted by
columns. The ceiling is
suspended from 3m deep
concealed steel I-beams that
span almost 30m across the
room.
Timber panelling is used
extensively below the first
floor gallery that runs along
three sides of the room.
Above this level, surfaces
are contrastingly smooth
and white: painted fibrous
plaster on the columns and
upper walls, lacquered
timber on the ceiling. They
help reflect light from
overhead lamps and the
central skylight. This works
something like a prism,
transmitting natural light
deep into the room without
admitting the sun's rays
directly.
The design of the skylight,
like so many of the building's
architectural features, is
based on circles and
squares.*

■ The 'stories' told in the various routes into Parliament House converge on the Members' Hall. Entry from all sides is signalled by four monumental portals. The ceremonial path from the north suggests a history of Australia which commences outside in Aboriginal aeons (Forecourt) and proceeds through Foyer and Great Hall to the present — suggested in the Members' Hall by the 'real-time' transient characteristics of the sky-lit atrium space and parliamentarians toing and froing. The Constitutional axis positions the two chambers on either side of the Members' Hall to express the bicameral nature of the Constitution. The Members' Hall is the literal and symbolic meeting place between the two Houses. The southerly Executive route has the Cabinet Room opening directly onto the Members' Hall. The Executive, which makes decisions affecting the nation, is seen to implement deliberations of the Houses to either side, while drawing on the advice of the people (in the committee rooms above), and on past experience (in the library on the top floor). The Executive axis intersects with the Constitutional axis (ensuring the rights of the people) and the ceremonial axis (its historical allegory a reminder of the impact of Cabinet decisions on national history and culture).

JG

■ *To pass through the portals that define the sides of the Members' Hall is to arrive at the centre of the building, and, symbolically, at the centre of Parliament and Australia. The symbolism is strengthened by the conjunction of three simple but potent images of Australia: the flag, the sky above, and parliamentarians below (collaging signs for patriotism, place, people). The four portals of the Members' Hall support the glazed canopy of the atrium roof. They take the historic form of a baldacchino (a canopy over a shrine or altar, usually held up by columns). At the centre of the space, directly under the flag, there is an altar-like object: a black granite-based pool reflecting the sky and the flag above (earth, sky, and water — all signs of place — are brought together with the flag — sign for 'Australia'). The fact that the portals are all the same helps unify the entries from four sides of Parliament House. The architectural theme of each entrance is a head-and-shoulders shaped opening. This anthropomorphic motif reminds all who enter the building that it is a place for and of the people. Around the Members' Hall this theme is repeated but on the monumental scale appropriate to the symbolic importance of this space as the centre of Parliament.*

■ *Architects' rendering (above); view up through small skylight to flag-mast (above right); detail of Federation Star (left).*

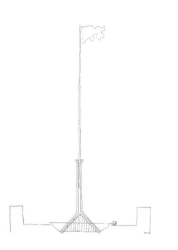

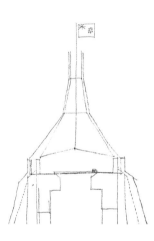

■ *Just what shape the flag-mast should be was the subject of much study. Above are two sketches made by the architects to test the extreme alternatives: a very high flagpole, and a very short one. Top right: the stainless steel leg sections ready for assembly. Centre: one of the legs being manoeuvred into position along the base of the curved wall. Below: lifting the flagpole.*

■ *Parliament's marker emblem, the flag-mast, was assembled from stainless steel plate. The plate used to fabricate the four triangular legs varies in thickness from 10mm to 36mm to account for the different stress levels in the structure. Although the legs appear to rest lightly on top of the curved walls, the total weight of the flag-mast is about 220 tonnes, and each leg is secured by 44 stainless steel bolts sunk 1.2m into the concrete. The tendency for the tops of the walls to spread is countered by tying them together with post-tensioned cables buried in the building's roof and spanning from east to west between each pair of legs. Holding together the pole and the vertical sections of the four legs are two hubs ('clusters'). For maintenance work, the clusters are reached in a three-person cage electrically driven on a track up the south-east leg. A smaller cage is operated to climb to the top of the pole. The overall height of the flag-mast is 81m. To minimize damage from Canberra's high winds, three flags are rotated, each flying for two weeks. They are 12.8 × 6.4m. Right: this massive temporary structure supported the four legs while the lower cluster tying them together was positioned.*

■ *The Senate chamber is smaller than the House of Representatives but more opulent. Furnishings — in Australian tonal variations of traditional Westminster red — appear richer, more regal than the opposite chamber's grey-greens. Dominating each space is a large ceiling canopy incorporating a prismatic glass skylight; the Senate version is elliptical and more elaborate than the angular design in the House. The same contrast of curved and rectilinear forms occurs in balustrades, staircases and other elements near the chambers.*

The structural carcase of the Senate is covered by fine finishes. Walls and ceiling are coated with white plasterglass. The dark red carpet is hand-tufted wool. Wool upholstered panels form a decorative dado to first floor height. The hand-dyed red tones become progressively lighter towards the ceiling.

MGT

■ *Red timber — jarrah from Western Australia — is used for seats, desks, doors, and the parquetry floor of areas surrounding the Senate chamber. Permanent seating is provided for 88 Senators and 20 advisers in the three-tiered horseshoe layout traditional to the British Houses of Parliament. Additional temporary seats can be installed on the third tier. At joint sittings of both Houses, up to 360 Members and Senators can be accommodated. The first floor galleries provide seating for 390 visitors and 75 journalists (who have offices nearby, although the building's four television studios are more centrally located near the Members' Hall on the ground floor). Public galleries also overlook the chamber from the second floor. These are glass-fronted and soundproofed to allow tour guides to explain proceedings below.*

135

■ When Australia's senators debate at night, evidence of the sessions is signalled to Canberra residents by the glowing light monitor projecting above the roof. This follows the tradition in Provisional Parliament House, where a red light shines over the Senate Chamber and a green light over the House of Representatives whenever the Houses are sitting. Like its counterpart above the House of Representatives chamber, the monitor works as a skylight during the day, casting constantly changing patterns of refracted light around the room.

The oval form of the chamber ceiling is repeated as curves cut out of the roof ridges. From across Canberra, this differentiates the Senate (with its circular geometry) from the House of Representatives on the other side of the building (with its more angular, square geometry). From outside, attention is drawn to the chamber roofs by their bright orange-red terra-cotta tiles, in vivid contrast to the otherwise neutral sandstone coloured finishes of Parliament House. The tiles are those used throughout suburban Australia. This architectural pun on 'house', with its everyday implications of ordinary people, underlines the Constitutional and symbolic significance of the people to Parliament House.

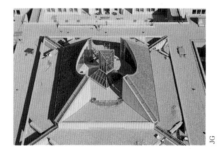

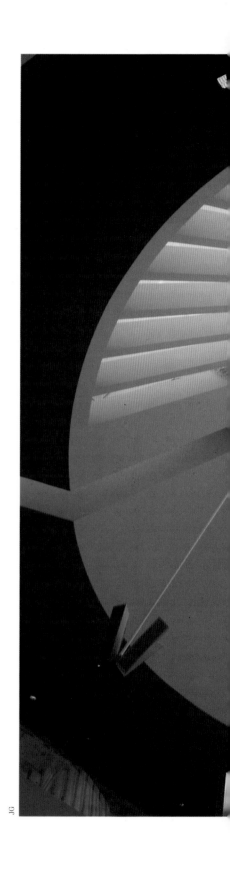

■ *Two architectural themes give each chamber ceiling an*
individual but related character: a contrasting geometry of circles
(Senate) and squares (House of Representatives); and columns.
The House ceiling is supported on paired columns; in the Senate,
'columns' of light hold the roof aloft.

■ *This page, clockwise from top right: selection of 'cippolino' marble at the quarry; Foyer column sleeves being fashioned from the 'cippolino' in Italy; the finished columns of 'cippolino' with bands of 'atlantide rosa'; white Carrara marble portico cladding; inspecting the Campanile quarry, Carrara; fixing Eugowra granite to the curved walls.*

■ *Tradition and public opinion demand for Parliament House the highest standards of craftsmanship and the most expensive materials, to create a building of substance as well as monumental presence. One of the strongest impressions of Parliament House is the richness of its finishes. Closer inspection, however, shows much of the building to be finished very simply.*

The trick is one of appearances. The most expensive materials are found where they will have greatest impact: not in the utilitarian spaces of the parliamentary office wings but in the public and ceremonial places. And even here these special materials are merely thin veneers, often just a few fine pieces of polished marble set in a much larger expanse of concrete and plaster.

Appropriately for Australia's constitutional monument, its finishes are an egalitarian mix of humble and rich materials. The architects' commitment has been to acquiring for the building a little of the very best: Carrara marble from northern Italy, Eugowra granite from western NSW. The contractors have matched this commitment by employing the finest craftsmen.

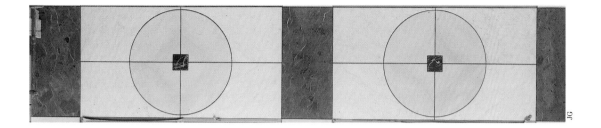

■ *This page, clockwise from*
top: marble inlay detail,
House of Representatives
chamber exterior; granite
outcrops, Eugowra,
quarried for the curved
walls; Foyer stairs.

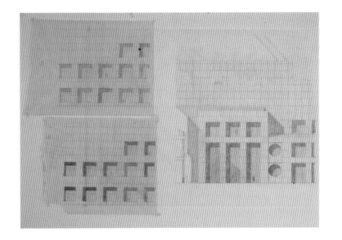

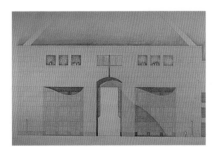

■ The final design of the curved walls was the result of much aesthetic and technical research. Many hundreds of preliminary study sketches were compared to test proportions, the effects of shadows, patterns of cladding joints, shapes for openings (top). The more successful options were then built as large-scale models to see what they would look like in three dimensions (centre), before detailed cladding studies were undertaken (bottom).

■ The curved walls are clad in 'carmina' granite from Eugowra, NSW, selected for its restrained, uniform appearance. Its pinkish tone is contrasted by panels of green 'verde issorie' marble at points where glazed links from the parliamentary wings connect.

Some 24,000 slabs of granite, averaging 1.5 × 1m in size and 50mm in thickness, were fixed to the concrete with stainless steel restraining pins and angle brackets. Because the architects sought a precise, flush finish, joints are the smallest feasible. These 6mm gaps are weatherproofed with recessed strips of neoprene rubber. All but the top and base stones are honed to a smooth finish. For stronger visual definition and added durability, the top and bottom edge courses are highly polished.

■ *Parliament House is defined by two strokes. They are sweeping arcs, like boomerangs back to back. The two curved walls establish the building's 'X' layout, frame its four entrance courts, support the flag-mast and reaffirm the axial geometry of Walter Burley Griffin's 1912 plan for Canberra. They are massive structures which seem deeply embedded in the hill.*

The walls are 450m long and rise in steps from 5m at the ends to approx 20m at their centres. Each is two skins of concrete which meet at the ends and spread apart in the centre to form a cavity which houses lifts, service installations and rooftop guard boxes. 'Windows' puncture each structure; these are designed to emphasize the cross plan of the building and are precisely made perpendicular to the north-south land axis, despite the changing aspects of the walls.

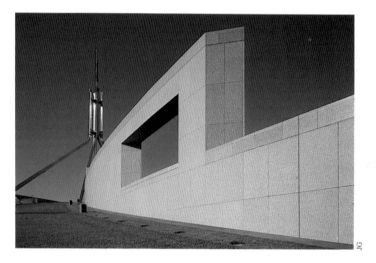

■ *The curved walls are the city-scaled emblems of Parliament House, the distant signs of human habitation on Capital Hill.*

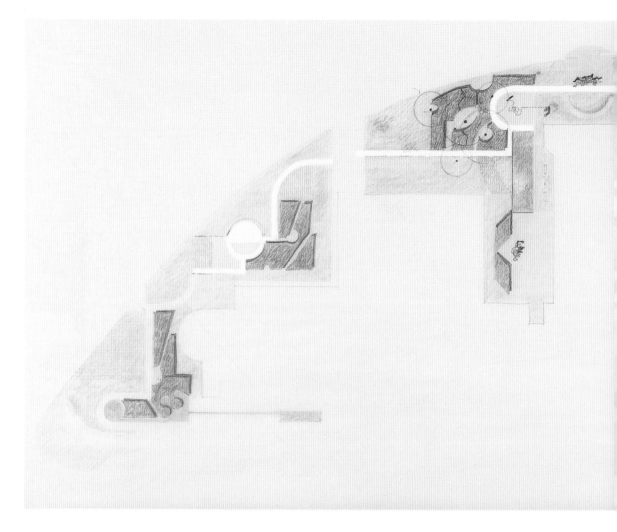

The space between the curved walls and the parliamentary wings has a distinctly urban scale: a broad curving 'street' lined with handsome civic buildings on one side and a continuous three-storey curving facade on the other. Romaldo Giurgola's early study for this space (top, dated mid-1982) identifies this 'urban' quality and develops a landscape design based on the formal civic garden with its regulating geometry, axes, reflecting pools, squares of paving, and regular planting beds. 'Courtyards' between buildings, such as the one for the House of Representatives Government Lobby (near right and centre), share a common vocabulary of materials and forms — yet each has its own character. Physically separated by pools, fountains, gardens, the courtyards are visually linked by a meandering path (far right). The landscaping design achieves the dignified, civic forms associated with important monuments and institutions, and at the same time satisfies the need for places to stroll, contemplate, or converse among peaceful settings. Landscaping for the curtilage of the Parliament House site is contrastingly bush-like.

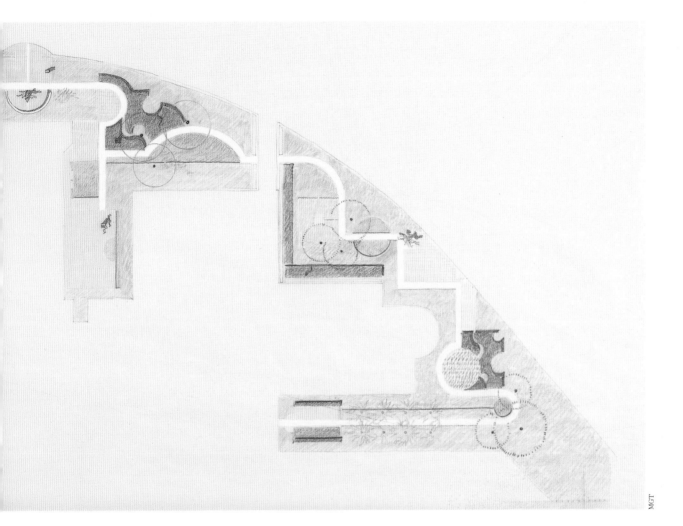

■ *The architects' rendering of the chamber. The roof is seen as a great canopy held up by paired columns at each corner. The columns also frame the public galleries, like a proscenium arch, and define the central space.*

■ *Parliamentary advisers must wait — often for long periods — outside the chamber in one of two spaces that have been made as diverting and congenial as possible. Proceedings inside the chamber can be glimpsed through the glazed corner. Balconies above are animated by constant comings and goings. Natural daylight prevents any sense of being confined here.*

■ *Although structurally similar, the House of Representatives (the people's House) has a different character from the Senate (the States' House). Decorated in grey-green shades of native gum leaves, its architecture is angular and appearance sober. The House has four pairs of corner columns supporting the prismatic roof with its central skylight (right). The chamber is identified externally by its distinctive terra-cotta roofs (centre right).*

The House has permanent seating for 170 Members, with room for another 190 temporary seats around the perimeter. Open first floor galleries seat 530 visitors. The second floor galleries are glazed and soundproofed for tour groups, translators, and broadcasters. Microphones at parliamentarians' desks are linked to stereo loudspeakers suspended from the ceiling, amplifying and locating debaters. Finishes are similar to those of the Senate, except in colour. The dominant timber is grey box, supplemented by turpentine. The carpet is dark green. Walls and ceiling are white. Upholstery materials are wool and leather. The restrained, austere atmosphere is also conveyed in the bas-relief coat of arms (bottom).

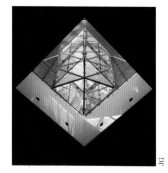

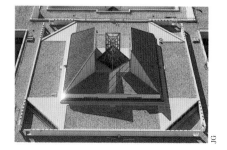

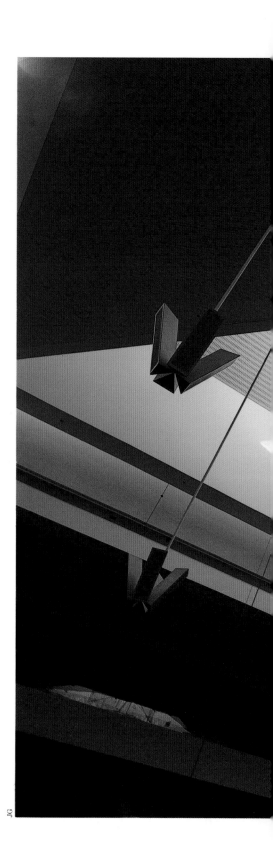

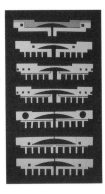

■ *The Senate President and the House Speaker each has a private courtyard. Clear architectural and iconographic distinctions are signalled in both. The President's Courtyard has red granite motifs and a magnificent arch (the architects' study models, above). Fine stone-like columns support the covered way to the Senate chamber. The Speaker's Courtyard is a plainer space, with square geometry and green marble inlays. Its covered way is conspicuously roofed in corrugated iron and supported on timber posts – like a house verandah.*

MINGARRI, THE LITTLE OLGAS

■ *Although of human height, the five bronzes in the Executive Courtyard are mountains. Marea Gazzard has named her work 'Mingarri — The Little Olgas' in a tribute to the range of rock forms seen from Ayers Rock in Australia's central desert. They were cast from plaster moulds taken from full-size clay models.*

Like the rock 'islands' in a Japanese Zen garden, 'Mingarri' is a serene focus in an austere landscape designed for contemplation. The Executive Courtyard is a private area for senior parliamentarians and guests. The Prime Minister's ground floor suite opens onto it, and here State visitors and the Prime Minister may stroll. Both the Executive Courtyard and the Forecourt have desert themes. But the Forecourt is an open sunburnt plain, while the Executive Courtyard is a Top End gorge: enclosed on all sides by high 'sandstone' walls, strewn with 'rocks', with leafy shade (from wisteria-draped pergolas) and a waterfall at one end feeding a small stream that flows across the stone paved floor. The Forecourt is a space for crowds to gather. The ' Executive Courtyard is a place for quiet reflection, with its pensive character enhanced by tinkling water and the changing plays of light and shadow.

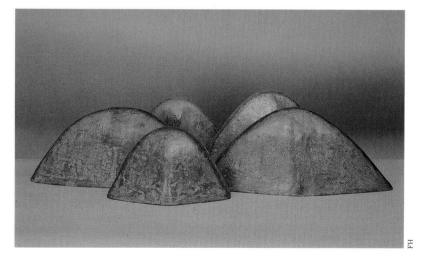

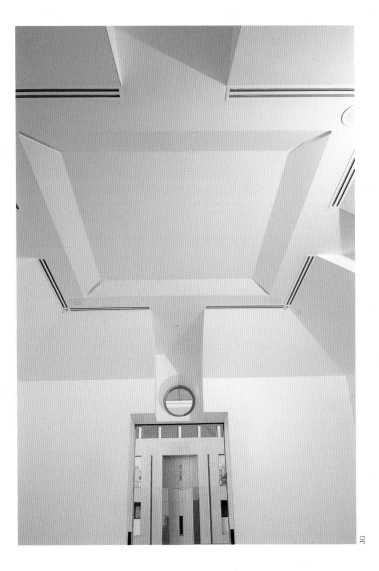

■ *The Prime Minister's suite opens directly onto the Executive Courtyard so that visiting dignitaries can drive right up to the 'front' door. The entrance lobby ceiling, like the rest of the suite, is austerely finished, with the emphasis on craftsmanship. The ceiling (above) has been skilfully modelled in fibrous plaster.*

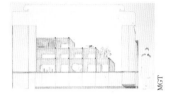

■ *The luxuriousness of the Prime Minister's suite is not overt:*
only the observant will note that the panelling is Huon pine —
Australia's most treasured timber. An area of about 700m²
incorporates a kitchen, bathroom, dining room (above), reception
area, and offices for the Prime Minister's personal staff.

157

■ *The Executive wing to the south of Parliament House is the private realm of the Prime Minister, Cabinet, and advisers. It is built on three levels around a cool courtyard with water and sculptures to encourage serene contemplation. The Prime Minister's suite opens directly to this space from the north and can be reached by car from the southern entrance. Ministers' suites, to east and west on the ground and first floors, overlook the garden but do not have direct access. Above them, on the second floor, is the 5,000m² Parliamentary Library, open to all parliamentarians and their staffs. Between the Prime Minister's suite and the Members' Hall is the Cabinet suite. Sophisticated security measures are taken here: the Cabinet Room essentially is a soundproof box inside a box, to allow security staff to check above the ceiling and behind the walls. To the west of the Cabinet suite are radio and television broadcasting studios, to the east the Media Library. Above are committee rooms where legislation is prepared. All the Executive spaces are necessarily close to the chambers: when the division bells sound, walking time from the furthest suite to either chamber is under two minutes; from the Cabinet Room it is around 40 seconds.*

AB

■ *The only painting
commissioned for hanging in
Parliament House is an
allegorical triptych by
Canberra artist Mandy
Martin. At 13m by 5m, it
almost fills the end wall of the
Main Committee Room, and
is now affectionately referred
to as 'The Big Picture'.
Another big picture, Tom
Roberts' realistic depiction of
the opening ceremony for
Australia's first Parliament
(painted from 1901 to 1903),
has been moved to the new
building, to hang at the
entrance to the Main
Committee Room. Its
composition, a crowd
arranged elliptically around
a stage, is echoed in Martin's
landscape of towering cliffs
and forbidding rocks
bordering an elliptical bay.
Although it is a coastal scene,
the ochre reds of the cliffs
recall Australia's deserts
more than its beaches.*

SH

■ *All the works commissioned for Parliament House deal with a sense of Australia as place, rather than focus literally on people or events. But Mandy Martin's painting, though a landscape, offers an allegory about the effects of people on the land.*
Several rocks in this painting (left in the main panel) seem man-made: these represent human interventions in nature. Dark clouds in the sky, black shadows in the foreground, and the unnatural colour of the sea all suggest that some interventions have been destructive.
The artist's vision does imply a more positive future: the dark skies are clearing. The Big Picture's focus is a diagonal shaft of sunlight piercing the thunder clouds.

161

■ *Apart from art and craft works commissioned specifically for the building, some 3,000 works — paintings, sculpture, craft objects, photographs — were purchased to form the Parliament Collection. These were chosen to complement the symbolic themes in Parliament House — principally, notions of the land: its Aboriginal people and ancient myths; its European settlement and exploration; its contemporary urban and rural development. The Collection is largely contemporary. However, it also includes important works from earlier periods.*

■ *Fred WILLIAMS 1927–82*
Trees and rocks I, 1963
tempera, oil on board
113×90cm

■ *Albert TUCKER born 1914*
Gold fossicker, 1955
oil on hardboard
62×53cm

■ *Arthur BOYD born 1920*
Riverbank, 1987
oil on canvas
152.5 × 146.6cm

■ *John OLSEN born 1928*
Sea Objects, 1973
acrylic on hardboard
125×121.3cm

■ *Anthony PRYOR born 1951*
Wall marker, 1982
mixed media
71.1 × 90.4 × 27cm

■ *Stephen BENWELL born*
Vase, 1983
earthenware
31.5 × 33.3cm diameter

■ *Elwyn LYNN born 1917*
Near Alice, 1981
acrylic, plaster on canvas
140 × 185cm

■ *Richard DUNN born 1944*
Untitled (Production and Red), 1983
pastel, charcoal on paper
226.8 × 230cm

■ *John, WOLSELEY born 1938*
From Bendigo to Kyoto in search of Basho, 1983–84
watercolour, pencil, ink, pastel, oil, paper on canvas
84.5×394.5 cm

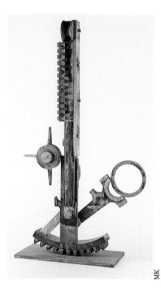

■ *Robert KLIPPEL born 1920*
Opus 537, 1985
painted and stained timber
202.5 × 113 × 42.5cm

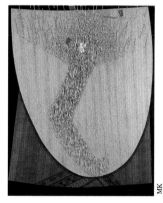

■ *John BRACK born 1920*
NO, 1984
oil on canvas
182.5 × 152cm

■ *Ann THOMSON*
Ritual, 1987
oil on canvas
182.6 × 197.7cm

■ *Sidney NOLAN born 1917*
Burke and Wills, 1964
oil on hardboard
122×122cm

163

AUTHORS AND PHOTOGRAPHER

Ivor Indyk earnt his doctorate at University College London for research on the theory of interpretation. He has been a Visiting Fellow at the Humanities Research Centre at the Australian National University, Canberra, and has taught at the University of Geneva, and the University of Sydney, where he now lectures on Australian literature.

Carl Andrew graduated from the School of Art at RMIT in 1960 and after working as a graphic designer in Melbourne he lived and painted on Rhodes for four years. On his return he studied Fine Arts at Melbourne University and directed the McClelland Gallery, Victoria. He was Curator of Art at the Tasmanian Museum and Art Gallery before moving to Sydney in 1980 to become Assistant Director, Decorative Arts, at the Powerhouse Museum.

Haig Beck left Brisbane for London in 1969 to complete his architecture studies at the Architectural Association School. In 1975 he became editor of Architectural Design and in 1979 launched International Architect with Jackie Cooper, editing and publishing the magazine until 1985. He returned to Australia in 1986 and is Senior Academic Associate at the University of Melbourne's Department of Architecture.

John Gollings, born 1944, studied architecture at the University of Melbourne. This training equipped him to become one of Australia's leading fashion photographers. However he increasingly discovered his time was being consumed by photographing buildings, since his interest in architectural theory and practice enables an overview that makes his pictures accessible to the public and critics alike.

CREDITS

Jane Adam (JA) 37

Anthony Browell (AB) Courtesy of Vogue Living Magazine 160, 161

Emery Vincent Associates (EV) 92, 93

Bernard Fisher (BF) 25, 33, 103

John Gollings (JG) 10, 12, 20, 21, 22, 23, 24, 25, 26, 27, 28, 29, 30, 31, 34, 42, 43, 47, 60, 62, 63, 66, 67, 70, 71, 72, 74, 75, 76, 77, 78, 87, 88, 91, 94, 95, 100, 101, 102, 103, 104, 105, 108, 109, 110, 111, 120, 122, 123, 124, 125, 126, 127, 129, 130, 131, 132, 133, 134, 135, 136, 137, 138, 139, 141, 142, 144, 145, 146, 147, 148, 149, 150, 151, 154, 156, 157, 158, 159, 165, 167, 168

Kate Gollings (KG) 165

Stephen Hall (SH) 8, 20, 30, 61, 126, 128, 138, 139, 160

Fenn Hincliffe (FH) Courtesy of Coventry Gallery, Sydney 39, 155

Ron Hinwood (RH) 38

Matt Kelso (MK) 162, 163

Michael Kluvanek (MK) 118

Kay Lawrence (KL) 119

Bernard Le Lievre (BLL) 59

Mitchell Giurgola Thorp (MGT) 32, 35, 36, 39, 40, 68, 69, 84, 85, 140

Ethel Perry (EP) 112

Debra Phillips (DP) 38, 82, 83

David Reid (DR) 79

Rollin/Franc (RF) 40, 64

Uffe Shultz (US) 38

David Simmonds (DS) 41, 112, 113

Victorian Tapestry Workshop (VTW) 116, 117

Aerial photographs of Capital Hill have been reproduced with the kind permission of the General Manager, Australian Surveying and Land Information Group, Department of Administrative Services, Canberra, 106, 107.

Illustrations by Anne Hooton (AH) 21, 22, 25, 26, 27, 28, 58, 60, 61

Marion Mahony Griffin's rendering of Walter Burley Griffin's winning design for the new capital (1912), Courtesy of the Australian National Library, Canberra, 15

ACKNOWLEDGEMENTS

'Australia's Parliament House', the book, was made in a matter of months while the building was still under construction. To say the least, this made life for the production team complicated. As editor, I would like to thank for their dedication and cheerful commitment:

Annelies Siero the designer, her assistant Anne Hooton, Ray Hatcher and Nicole Rasmussen for finished artwork, Ian Hughes who co-ordinated the typesetting, and the architects Graham Jahn and George Kringas for use of their office; Davina Jackson researched and wrote captions, Jackie Cooper sub-edited and proofread texts, and Michael Wyatt prepared the index; at the Watermark Press, Alexandra Towle and Simon Blackall supervised printing and binding; and at the NSW Chapter of the Royal Australian Institute of Architects, it was Chris Johnson's task to liaise and inspire.

In Canberra at the Parliament House Construction Authority, special thanks to Bernard Shirley, Stephen Hall and Dianna Harvey at Mitchell/Giurgola & Thorp, to Pamille Berg, Hal Guida, and their colleagues; and on site at the Concrete-Holland Joint Venture, to David Chandler, Noëla Horsley, Richard Roberts, and Jack Kershaw.

Haig Beck

Many organizations participated in the construction of Parliament House.

On the following pages are listed those organizations which had a trade or works contract with the Parliament House Construction Authority and were, in general, managed by the Construction Manager — Concrete-Holland Joint Venture.

For each contractor, the location of their works is indicated as follows:

  — North area; S — South area; W — West area; E — East area; G — Global (throughout the building);   — Peripheral (site works and landscaping)

AC SHEETING PTY LTD	Supply fibre cement	G
A E ATHERTON & SON PTY LTD	Supply exhaust hoods & service spines	G
AARQUE SYSTEMS PTY LTD	Document reproduction	P
ABA INTERNATIONAL DIV OF HABLIP PTY LTD	Car park boom gates	P
ABC ENGINEERING SERVICE & CONSTRUCTION GROUP	Sound & vision systems	G
ARC/HUMES ENGINEERING PTY LTD	Supply steel reinforcement	N,S,E,W,P
ACCESS HARDWARE PTY LTD	Supply door hinges	G
ACT ELECTRICITY AUTHORITY	Power supply	G
ADVANX TYRE & RUBBER CO PTY LTD	Supply of bearing pads	N,W
AGL CANBERRA LTD	Incoming gas main	P
AINSWORTH & BURTON PTY LTD	Media & computer fitouts police posts to curved walls	W,G
ALCAN AUSTRALIA LTD	Supply aluminium window sections	G
ALIMAK AUSTRALIA PTY LTD	Flagmast access system	N
ALL-FAB CONSTRUCTIONS PTY LTD	Metalwork & structural steel	N,E,G
ALLEN TAYLOR & CO LTD	Timber supply	G
ALPINE NURSERIES	Supply miscellaneous plants	G
ALTONE TRAFFIC EQUIPMENT MANUFACTURER PTY LTD	On-air signs, monumental clocks & foyer pendant structure	G
AMDEL (NSW DIVISION)	Testing fire proofing material	G

ANI PERKINS	Emergency generators	G
AQUILA STEEL AND CO	Reinforcement steel	E,W
ASAD SIGNS — A DIVISION OF MANGROVE PTY LTD	Supply exit signs	G
ATCO STRUCTURES (QLD)	Site establishment	P
ATELIER FURNITURE & INTERIORS PTY LTD	Chamber seats & desks	E,W
AUSTREOFIX PTY LTD	Reinforcement fixing	N,S
AUSTRESS PTY LTD	Post-tensioning	W
AVANT GARDEN HORTICULTURAL ENTERPRISES	Garden maintenance	P
B & K STEELFIXING PTY LTD	Reinforcement fixing	N,S
E A BAILEY & SONS PTY LTD	Waffle infill panels	N,W,G
BALMORAL ENGINEERING PTY LTD	Irrigation control system	P
BAXTER ENGINEERING PTY LTD	Supply of metal work & handrails	S,W,G
BBC HARDWARE	Supply of door closers, accessories & soap dispensers	G
BBR AUSTRALIA PTY LTD	Pre-stressing & post-tensioning	N,S,W
BELLS THERMALAG & INDUSTRIAL SERVICES	Fire protection of structural steelwork	N
BENMAX PTY LTD	Supply & install metal plinth frames, mechanical services	N,S,G
BERKELEY CHALLENGE PROPERTY SERVICES PTY LTD	Internal cleaning	E,W
BINK CEMENT PRODUCTS	Precast vehicle buffers	W
BLUE METAL & GRAVEL PTY LTD	Concrete supply	G
BORAL SGB PTY LTD	Scaffolding & waffle pan supply	G
BOWSERS ASPHALT	Fire proofing & sealing of penetrations	G
BREAKTHRU DEMOLITION	Supply timber for pergolas	G
BRIDGEWATER TRADING & ENGINEERING PTY LTD	External metal-clad doors	G
BROOKS MARCHANT IND (ACT) PTY LTD	Mechanical services	N
BUNNING BROS PTY LTD	Architectural woodwork supply	G
BYRNE & DAVIDSON DOORS (NSW) PTY LTD	Fire rated shutters	G
C E INDUSTRIES	Supply bearing pads & elastomeric pads	S,E,W
CAMERON & JASON PTY LTD	Airboxes, grilles & balustrades to glazed links	W
CANBERRA CERAMIC TILES PTY LTD	Wall & floor coverings	N,S,E,W,G
CANBERRA PAVING SERVICE PTY LTD	Concrete placing & finish	N,S,E,W
CANFAB ENGINEERING PTY LTD	External metalwork & steel bicycle racks, camera masts & bollards	G,P
CAPITAL CIVIL	Excavations, car park paving & backfill	P
CECON LIMITED	Dry wall partitions & general ceilings	E
CITRA CONSTRUCTIONS LTD	Carpentry & joinery, flag mast installation, landscaping & associated construction work	N,S,G,P
CON-DRILL (ACT)	Concrete sawing & drilling	G
COYLE F R PTY LTD	Suspended hydraulics	E,W,P
CAPITAL DRYLINING PTY LTD	Soffit lining, plaster walling & ceilings	N,E,W
CAPITAL STEEL FIXING CONTRACTORS	Reinforcement fixing	S,E,W
CHANNON REFRIGERATION PTY LTD	Beverage reticulation system	G
CHUBB AUSTRALIA LIMITED	Special security doors, locking system & installation of fire extinguishers	G
CIVIC STEEL FIXING	Reinforcement fixing	E,W,P
CO DESIGN (A DIVISION OF FELTEX COMMERCIAL INTERIORS PTY LTD)	Supply & installation of office systems	G
COFFEY & PARTNERS PTY LTD	Concrete testing	G
COMALCO FABRICATIONS LTD	Windows	S,W
COONEY REFRIGERATION PTY LTD	Coldrooms — fabrication, erection & commissioning	G
CONDITIONED AIR PTY LTD	Maintenance of air conditioning services	G
CONSIDINE, D W & SONS PTY LTD	Supply of ferrules & sleeves	G
CORKHILL BROS SALES PTY LTD	Soil works	P
CORPORATE CARPET INSTALLATION SERVICE	Manufacture & installation of carpets	N,S,G
CSIRO	Various testing — windows membrane	G
D NORMOYLE & CO PTY LTD	Structural steel & metalwork	N,S,G
D P FORMWORK	Inspection pits	N
DANBY-O'CONNOR PARLIAMENT HOUSE JOINT VENTURE	Carpentry & joinery	S,E,W
DAVRO SERVICES	Inward goods conveyor system	G
DELAIRCO CONTRACTING PTY LTD	Electrical services	S
DEPARTMENT OF ADMINISTRATIVE SERVICES	Storage of materials	P
DOLSO CONSTRUCTIONS PTY LTD	Formwork	E,W
DUNCAN'S HOLDINGS LTD	Timber supply	G
EPM CONCRETE PTY LTD	Precast concrete	N,E,W,G
E BECKMAN & CO PTY LTD	General metalwork	N,S,E
EASTCO CONSTRUCTION PTY LTD	Concrete retaining wall & erection of panels	S, G
EBIR BY ZAROCK	Site establishments	P
EMAIL AIR HANDLING	Maintenance of air filters	G
EMAIL LTD	Supply of dishwashers	G
ESTABLISHED TREE PLANTERS PTY LTD	Supply & growing of trees	P
FAVELLE CRANES & SERVICES PTY LTD	Supply of tower cranes	G
FAVCO CRANES	Supply of tower cranes	G

FIRE CONTROL PTY LTD	Fire doors & frames	N,S,E,W,G
FLAT TOP ROOFING CO PTY LTD	Roof membrane & tanking	N,E,W,G
FFE ALDRIDGE (ELECTRICAL) PTY LTD	Electrical services	W,G
FLICK W A & CO PTY LTD	Vermin control	G,P
FORM-IT FIBREGLASS	Supply of waffle pans	W
FRANKPILE AUSTRALIA	Bored piers	E,W,G
GEC AUSTRALIA	Luminaires	G
GATIC (AUST) PTY LTD	Rainwater outlets	P
GEELONG FABRICATIONS PTY LTD	Glazed links & supportive structures	N,E,W
GEO TALL & CO PTY LTD	Supply egress bolts	G
G HIGGINS COATING	Painting	E
GLENCOR CONSTRUCTIONS PTY LTD	Cleaning curved wall	G
GOLDER ASSOCIATES PTY LTD	Testing concrete & materials	P
GRANITES OF AUSTRALIA PTY LTD	Granite, dressing & erection to curved walls	G
GRANOR RUBBER ENGINEERING CO	Bearing pads	N,S
GRABER SUPPLIES	Roof outlets & inspection pits	N,S,W,P
GREGORYS PLUMBING & PIPELINE SERVICES	Temporary hydraulics	P
HONEYWELL LIMITED	Security alarm system	G
HUGHES BROS PTY LTD	Co-ordinated finishes to main entry, Members' & Guests' Dining Room, Prime Minister's and Cabinet. Co-ordinated finishes & general joinery to cooling tower	N,S,P
H T WATERPROOFING CONTRACTORS PTY LTD	Tanking & membrane	N,W,G,P
H & J ARCHITECTURAL PRODUCTS PTY LTD	Special exterior doors, main entry doors & windows	N,G
HARRISON, ROY PTY LTD	Conduiting & cable trays	P
HAWKER ROOFING	Expansion joint covers	P
HERCULES ENGINEERING	Bearing pads	P
HERTZ ELECTRONICS PTY LTD	Clock system & divisional lights	G
HORNET REINFORCEMENT	Reinforcement fixing	E
HYDRANT & SPRINKLER INSTALLATION SERVICES	Fire sprinkler system	S
INTERSEEN PTY LTD	Construction of reinforced concrete transition slab, corbel, screeds & granolithic floor finishes	N,S,E,W,G
INTALITE PTY LTD	Luminaires	G
IVAN & SON ACT PTY LTD	Electrical works & lighting	N,S
JAYBEE ENGINEERING PTY LTD	General waste system	G
JOHNS PERRY LIFTS	Lift services	N,S,G
J M F PAINTERS PTY LTD	Painting	S,W
JOHN HOSKINS PTY LTD	External backfill, inground hydraulics	N,S,G,P
K S FREIGHTERS	Transport of precast panels	W
KELL & RIGBY (BUILDERS) PTY LTD	Co-ordinated finishes & joinery to Senate & House chambers	E,W
KILPATRICK GREEN PTY LTD	Electrical services	W,G,P
KAYDA (AUST) PTY LTD	Painting	N,S
KEELER HARDWARE (ACT) PTY LTD	Hardware consultancy	G
KELL & DENSON PTY LTD	Saw pavers & prototype stone	P
KENNEDY CLEANING SERVICES PTY LTD	Internal cleaning	E
KENNEDY & TAYLOR (NSW) PTY LTD	Temporary electrical services	G,P
KERRY, N W PTY LTD	Suspended hydraulics	W
LENSLITE PTY LTD TRADING AS HOLOPHONE AUSTRALIA	Luminaires	G
LIMRO CLEANING SERVICES	Cleaning offices	P
LUMO CONSTRUCTIONS PTY LTD	Formwork, interim miscellaneous works & contract labour tradeworks	N,S,G
LAMSON ENGINEERING AUSTRALIA PTY LTD	Pneumatic tube system, document moving system	G
LAND INDUSTRIES	Landscaping	P
LIDI AUSTRALIA PTY LTD	Supply & install vertical blinds & wooden venetian blinds	G
LUKE AIR CONDITIONING	Mechanical services — chillers	G
LYSAGHT STAINLESS	Stainless steel for flagmast	N,S
MATTHEW HALL PTY LTD	Mechanical & electrical services, fire protection	N,S,E,W,P
MELOCCO LIMITED	Stonework & granite	N,S,E,G
METZ & COMPANY PTY LTD	Kitchen wall & floor tiling	N,S,W
MIMELLIS, T	Site catering	P
MITSIKAS BROS & COMPANY	Steelfixing	E,G
MONIER LTD	Black granite quarrying, supply of red granite	G
MORRIS, A G & A M	Grey/pink granite quarrying and pavers	G
MOTOROLA ELECTRONICS AUSTRALIA PTY LTD	Mobile radio and distributed aerial system	G
MURRAY AMPLIFIERS	Microphone amplifier & co-ordination	G
NALTY PTY LTD TRADING AS R K JOINERY	Printroom joinery	E
NATIONAL NEON SIGNS	Luminaires	G
NILSEN ELECTRIC (SA) PTY LTD	Area main switchboards	G
NIRA AUSTRALIA PTY LTD	Pocket paging system	G

NORTHERN CONTRACTORS PTY LTD	Media fitout	W
O'NEILL & BROWN PLUMBING CO. PTY LTD	Suspended hydraulics	N,S,E
OLEX CABLES LTD	Supply of irrigation control wiring	P
OLIVER-DAVEY GLASS CO PTY LTD	Glazing	E
PIONEER CONCRETE (SA) PTY LTD	Precast concrete	S,W
PACIFIC COMMUNICATIONS (SALES) PTY LTD	Security closed circuit television system	G
PACIFIC WASTE MANAGEMENT	Waste disposal	G
PANGALLO, M PTY LTD	Render and plaster work	N,S
PANICH, BOB CONSULTANCY	Spotlights, engineering & drafting for winching systems	G
PEGLER HATTERSLEY AUST PTY LTD	Suspended hydraulics	N
PEKON FIRE PROTECTION PTY LTD	Fire sprinklers	W,G,P
PFEIFFER, JOHN	Concrete placing	P
PHILIPS COMMUNICATIONS SYSTEMS LTD	Security screening devices	G
PHILIPS SCIENTIFIC AND INDUSTRIAL	House monitoring system equipment	G
PLEASURE PLANTS WHOLESALE NURSERY	Supply plants for landscaping	G
POOL TECHNOLOGY AUST PTY LTD	Fountain pumproom equipment	G
PORTACOM	Site establishments	P
PREFABRICATED CONCRETE & TERRAZZO (VIC) PTY LTD	Terrazzo stairs and landings	E,W
PRESTRESSING CONCRETE AUSTRALIA PTY LTD	Expansion joint seals	W
PROFAB INDUSTRIES PTY LTD	General metalwork	E,W
PROJECT LIGHTING PTY LTD	Luminaires & powered signs	G
RIDGE CONSOLIDATED	Reinforced earth wall	N
RINTOUL PTY LTD	Carpentry, joinery & co-ordinated finishes to Reception & Members' Hall & the theatrette	N,E,W
RIZZOLO STONE & CONCRETE PTY LTD	Supply of sandstone	P
ROCHE BROS PTY LTD	Landscaping, inground hydraulics & bulk excavation, Forecourt finishes	G,P
ROSEK & BRODZORIC PTY LTD	Concrete placing	W
RAYMOR (CANBERRA) PTY LTD	Sanitary fittings	G
RENO PTY LTD	Blockwork	E
RHAM INDUSTRIES PTY LTD	Supply luminaires	G
H H ROBERTSON PTY LTD	Skylights & roof monitors	N,E,W,G
ROPAKS DEVELOPMENT PTY LTD	Formwork	S,E,W,P
ROVERA CONSTRUCTIONS	Scaffolding	E,G
RYMER LIGHTING PTY LTD	Lighting & office luminaires	G
SABEMO PTY LTD	Eastern car park & loading dock	P
SAVO STANKOVICH PTY LTD	Landscaping	P
SHELLEY, R & G PTY LTD	Car park	G
SYSTEMS JOINTING PTY LTD	Vehicle buffers, waterproofing, sealants, epoxy fill & grit blasting	G
SEAL REINFORCEMENTS PTY LTD	Miscellaneous steelfixing	G
SELECTED LOCK & HARDWARE PTY LTD	Door hardware	G
SEXTON LOW TRADING CO PTY LTD	Manufacture & install hand tufted carpets	G
SHARWOOD STONE PTY LTD	Internal stone paving & stone fixing	S,E
SPECIALITY HARDWARE SERVICES	Miscellaneous door hardware	G
SPF FORMWORK PTY LTD	Formwork	W
SPRAY GRASS SERVICES PTY LTD	Landscaping	P
SPRINGVALE NURSERIES	Supply of plants	P
STAFF LIGHTING (AUST) PTY LTD	Centre zone roof uplights	G
STRATHAYR INSTANT LAWN	Supply of turf	P
STROUD INDUSTRIES	Painting	S
STEEL-LINE INDUSTRIES	Non fire rated shutters	G
STRUCTURAL CONCRETE SYSTEMS PTY LTD	Post-tensioning links	W
SUNSET PTY LTD	Supply of access road pavers	P
SUPERLINE PLASTIC PRODUCTS	Luminaires	G
TABLEHANDS PLUMBING SUPPLIES PTY LTD	Suspended hydraulics	P
TASMANIAN BRICKLAYING SERVICES	Blockwork	S,W
TECH LITE PTY LTD	Supply of special exit & broadcast signs	G
TERRAZZO & CO PTY LTD	Toilet partitions & doors	N,S,E,W
TERRAZZO TILES INDUSTRIES PTY LTD	Stonework & staircase	S,E,W
TESTCRETE LABORATORIES PTY LTD	Testing of concrete & material testing service	P
THIESS CONTRACTORS PTY LTD	Bulk earthworks & inground hydraulics	G
THYCON SYSTEMS PTY LTD	Emergency lighting supply units	G
TIMALCO GLASS STRUCTURES PTY LTD	Windows & links doors	G
TOM STODDART (DISTRIBUTORS) PTY LTD	Major kitchen equipment, supply & installation stainless steel works, bar equipment & installation and entry gates	N,G
TOP STAGE PRODUCTIONS	Luminaires	G
TORRENS INDUSTRIES PTY LTD	Building monitoring system	G
TOWNSEND C D CONTRACTING PTY LTD	Suspended metal ceiling	W
TURNER BROS FURNISHINGS PTY LTD	Curtains and motorised sunscreens	G
TYREE ELECTRICAL PTY LTD	Supply of transformers	G

UNIDRILL PTY LTD	Bored piers	P
UNISEARCH LIMITED	Membrane & roof testing	G
UNITED CARPET MILLS PTY LTD	Carpets	E
VISIN PTY LTD TRADING AS FABCON	Internal precast panels	N
VISLON PTY LTD	Render and plaster	N,S,E,W
VSL PRESTRESSING (AUST)	Post-tensioning	N
WALCO GROUP	Building hoists	G
WARD CIVIL ENGINEERING PTY LTD	Landscaping & roadworks	E,G,P
WATSON, R M SERVICES PTY LTD	Minor building	P
WODEN CONSTRUCTIONS PTY LTD	Bituminous pavement	W
WOLLONGONG CONSTRUCTIONS PTY LTD	Landscaping & earthworks	P
WILDRIDGE & SINCLAIR ENGINEERING PTY LTD	Mechanical Services	N,S
WILLIAM EDMUND PTY LTD	Suspended & inground hydraulics	S,W
WILSON FLOORS PTY LTD	Resilient flooring	N,E,W
WILSON INDUSTRIES PTY LTD	Dry walls & ceilings	S
WORMALD INTERNATIONAL (AUST) PTY LTD	Fire protection	N,W
YARRALUMLA NURSERY	Supply of plants	P

ADDITIONAL CONSULTANTS

BOOTLE, KEITH	Timber consultant
FORBES, DAVID	Fabric consultant
TRAVIS, PETER	Colour consultant

The following list is as complete as possible at the time of printing.

Agents, consultants, non-building item contractors and Art Programme commissions.

Where two or more people collaborated on a project they are listed as in the contract rather than alphabetically.

ACT ELECTRICITY AUTHORITY	Power supply
ADEB PTY LTD	Furniture
A T HEIGHES & SON (AUST)	Basement signs
ALAN PAYNE & PARTNERS PTY LTD	Flag hoisting consultant
ALEXANDER J COOK PTY LTD	Furniture
ALTONE (DIVISION OF TRAFFIC EQUIPMENT MANUFACTURERS PTY LTD)	Signs
ANDREW SWEENEY	Sound, vision, design and engineering support
ANDREWS, GORDON/HINWOODS, ROB & RHYLL	House of Representatives coat of arms fabrication
ANSETT TECHNOLOGIES	Furniture
ARMM CONSULTANTS INC	Roofing consultant
ARTES STUDIOS PTY LTD	Furniture
ASSOCIATION OF CONSULTING ENGINEERS FOR NEW PARLIAMENT HOUSE (ACEPH): Joseph R Loring & Associates; Norman Disney & Young; WE Basset & Partners Pty Ltd; Ledingham Hensby Oxley & Partners Pty Ltd	Services consultant
ATELIER FURNITURE AND INTERIORS PTY LTD	Furniture
AUSTRALIAN BROADCASTING CORPORATION (ABC)	Sound and vision systems
AUSTRALIAN MINERAL DEVELOPMENT LABORATORIES (AMDL)	Stonework consultant
BAC AUSTRALIAN SYSTEMS PTY LTD	Furniture
BASSETT FURNITURE PTY LTD	Furniture
BEMAC LABORATORIES PTY LTD	Concrete technology consultant
BISHOP, TONY/RETTER, MICHAEL	Marquetry
BLACKLOW, ROBERT	Senate chamber furniture
BLACK, HENRY	Foyer display case
BLAU, ROBIN	Coats of arms for Executive entry and Great Verandah
BROWNBUILT PTY LTD	Furniture
CAHILL, MAUREEN/LARSEN, HELGE	Suspended light fittings
CANBERRA ART FRAMING CO	Mountboard for art works
CANBERRA PLAN PRINTING AND COPY CENTRE	Plan printing
C D TOWNSEND (ENG) PTY LTD	Furniture
CELESTIAL PRODUCTS PTY LTD	Furniture
CHANNON REFRIGERATION PTY LTD	Beverage reticulation
CMS COLLABORATIVE	Water feature consultant
CO-DESIGN (DIVISION OF FELTEX COMMERCIAL INTERIORS PTY LTD)	Furniture
COFFEY & PARTNERS PTY LTD	Geotechnical consultant

COMMERCIAL INDUSTRIES PTY LTD	Furniture
COMMERCIAL KITCHEN CONSULTANTS PTY LTD	Refreshment services design
CONCRETE-HOLLAND JOINT VENTURE	Construction Director
CORDWELL, E	Huon pine
CRUICKSHANK, LISE	Rugs
DANISH DELUXE AUSTRALIA PTY LTD	Furniture
DANISH QUALITY FURNITURE PTY LTD	Furniture
DAVELL PRODUCTS SALES PTY LTD	Furniture
DAVRO FOSTER FURNITURE MANUFACTURERS PTY LTD	Furniture
DAVRO SERVICES	Conveyor system
DEPARTMENT OF ADMINISTRATIVE SERVICES	Transport and installation of furniture/Security consultant
DEPARTMENT OF COMMUNICATIONS AND TRANSPORT	Radio frequency planning
DERMER, JOHN	Ceramic urns
DONALD CANT, WATT, HAWES & LEE PTY LTD	Quantity surveyor
DOWIE, JOHN	Sculpture of HM Queen Elizabeth II
DUMBRELL, LESLEY	Design of rugs
DUNLOP, ROBERT	Table and chairs for Great Hall
EMAIL (AUST) PTY LTD	Dishwashers
EMBROIDERERS' GUILDS OF AUSTRALIA	Embroidery for Great Hall
EMERY, DAVID	House of Representatives Speaker's suite furniture
EMERY VINCENT ASSOCIATES PTY LTD	Graphics design
EPITYPE PTY LTD	Graphics typeface font production
EXHIBIT RESOURCES PTY LTD	Furniture
FACILITIES DEVELOPMENT	Furniture
FACILITIES MANAGEMENT PTY LTD	Data management
FERGUSON, ANNE	Foyer finials
FINEDESIGN FURNITURE	Leader of the Opposition's suite furniture
FINI FRAMES PTY LTD	Art works framing
FIRTH-SMITH, JOHN	Design of rug for House of Representatives Advisers' Waiting Space
FORSTER, HENDRIK	Sundial
GAZZARD, MAREA	Sculpture for Ministerial Courtyard
GEC/PHILIPS OPERA HOUSE LIGHTING CO PTY LTD	Lighting consultant
GEO A POCKETT & ASSOCIATES	Furniture
GEORGE SEXTON ASSOCIATES	Lighting consultant
GILL, MICHAEL	Furniture
G J HARRISON PTY LTD	Furniture
GRUNDY, PROFESSOR P/SCHMIDT, PROFESSOR L C	Flagmast elastic stability consultants
HAMILTONS PTY LTD	Furniture
HERSCHELL STENT PTY LTD	Furniture
HONEYWELL AUSTRALIA LTD	Security alarm system
HORTON, EDE	Stained glass
HTS INDUSTRIES PTY LTD	Furniture
IRRIGATION DESIGN CONSULTANTS	Irrigation consultant
IRWIN JOHNSTON & PARTNERS	Structural engineering consultant
JAMES BRADLEY'S PTY LTD	Furniture
JAYBEE ENGINEERING PTY LTD	Central waste movement systems
JOHNS PERRY LIFTS	Flagmast access consultant
JOHNS PERRY LTD	Steel pre-order consultant
JONES, NOLA	Rug design
KEE, JENNY	Rug design
KEELER HARDWARE PTY LTD	Architectural hardware consultant
K & S LYONS (VIC) PTY LTD	Furniture
KINHILL ENGINEERS PTY LTD	Furniture procurement consultant
KOKER, BERNIE (CONSTANTIA)	House of Representatives table and desk
KORDA, ERIC	Prime Minister's suite rug
LANGLEY, WARREN	Stained glass and sculpture
LAMSON ENGINEERING AUSTRALIA PTY LTD	Document movement systems
LAWRENCE, KAY	Prime Minister's suite tapestry/Great Hall embroidery, design and co-ordination
LEACH-JONES, ALUN	Rug design
LIGHTMAKERS PTY LTD	Lamps
LOUIS A CHALLIS & ASSOCIATES PTY LTD	Consulting acoustical and vibration engineers
LYNX FURNITURE	Furniture
McINTOSH, WILLIAM	Fabrication of Forecourt mosaic
McELHINNY, CHRIS	Senate President's suite furniture

McLACHLAN GROUP PTY LTD	Project planner
MARTIN, MANDY	Main Committee Room painting
MAUNSELL & PARTNERS PTY LTD	Civil Engineering consultant
MELBOURNE, PROFESSOR WILLIAM	Wind consultant
METLAB MAPEL PTY LTD	Welding inspection
MILTON, FRANK	Fees consultant
MITCHELL/GIURGOLA & THORP ARCHITECTS	Architects
MOTOROLA ELECTRONICS AUSTRALIA PTY LTD	Mobile radio system
MSS ALARM SYSTEMS PTY LTD	Store security
NETTLETON, LIZ	Rugs
NEW STYLE FURNITURE PTY LTD	Furniture
NIRA AUSTRALIA PTY LTD	Pocket paging system
NORTHCOTE POTTERY PTY LTD	Planters
OLDFIELD AND DANIEL	Miscellaneous equipment
OLIVER, LAURIE	House of Representatives furniture
O & O SYSTEMS CONSULTANTS PTY LTD	Cost and data support services
ORCHARD SCULPTURE FURNITURE	Furniture
OSTERGAARD, EGON & GRETHE	Furniture and woodworking consultant
PACHUCKA, EWA	Sculptural installation, House of Representatives Lobby Courtyard
PACIFIC COMMUNICATION SALES PTY LTD	Closed-circuit television system
PANCZAK & WILLENBERG	Cabinet suite tables
PARKER FURNITURE PTY LTD	Furniture
PERKINS, KEVIN	Prime Minister's suite, furniture and panelling
PETER F DANBY	Furniture
PETER G ROLLAND & ASSOCIATES	Landscape architect
PHILIPS	Security screening devices
PHILLIP SILVER	Furniture
PHILLIPS, CHERRY	Stained glass
PLANET PRODUCTS	Furniture
PLUTO FURNITURE SALES PTY LTD	Furniture
PUMP & CRANK PTY LTD	Furniture
RAMSDEN, MICHAEL/OLDROYD, GRAHAM	Members' Hall ceramic mural
RAWLINSON, ROBERTS & ASSOCIATES PTY LTD	Cost planners
RIJSDIJK, MEZZA	Stained glass
RINTOUL PTY LTD	Furniture
ROBERT WOODWARD PTY LTD	Water features consultant
ROLF JENSEN & ASSOCIATES INC	Life safety consultant
RUSSO, ANTHONY/WEICHARDT, MARK	Display cases
SCOTT & FURPHY ENGINEERS PTY LTD	Earthworks consultant
SEBEL FURNITURE LTD	Furniture
SEDGWICK PTY LTD	Insurance consultant
SMITH, JOHN	Leader of the Opposition's suite furniture
STAPLETON, BRIAN	Cost reporting
TAYLOR, PETER	Design of Senate Chamber coat of arms
TELECOM AUSTRALIA	Communication systems
TJAKAMARRA, MICHAEL NELSON	Design of Forecourt mosaic
T & K GLASS	Glass table tops
TOM STODDART (DISTRIBUTORS) PTY LTD	Kitchen equipment
TROPITONE FURNITURE	Furniture
TYREE ELECTRICAL CO PTY LTD	Transformers
UPFILL-BROWN, DAVID	House of Representatives Speaker's chair
VICTORIAN TAPESTRY WORKSHOP/BOYD, ARTHUR	Tapestry for Great Hall
VAUGHAN, GRANT	Display cases
WANG COMPUTERS PTY LTD	Security equipment
W L JACKSON & SONS	Furniture
WILLIAMS, CAMERON	Ceramic urns
WILLIAMS, EVAN	Rare timber
WILLIAMS, LYN	Fred Williams paintings
WILLIAMS, WILLIAM	Members' Hall display cases
WOODMARK FURNITURE PTY LTD	Furniture
WRIGHT, DAVID	Stained glass windows
WYCOMBE INDUSTRIES	Furniture
ZIMMER, KLAUS	Stained glass windows